The design of lighting

The design of lighting

Peter Tregenza and David Loe

E & FN SPON
An Imprint of Routledge

London and New York

Published by E & FN Spon, an imprint of Routledge,
11 New Fetter Lane, London EC4P 4EE

Simultaneously published in the USA and Canada
by Routledge
29 West 35th Street, New York, NY 10001

First edition © 1998 Peter Tregenza and David Loe

Typeset in 9.5/13pt Optima by Fox Design, Godalming, Surrey
Printed in Hong Kong by Dah Hua Press Co. Ltd

British Library Cataloguing in Publication Data
A catalogue record for this book is available from the British Library

ISBN 0 419 20440 7

Contents

List of tables

Preface

This book is an introduction to lighting in buildings, written for architects, interior designers and building services engineers. It is planned to be a reference for practitioners and a text-book for students. It covers daylighting and electric lighting, and introduces the use of colour.

There are three parts. The first, **The Technical Background**, gives the framework of physical and human factors used by the lighting designer: the ways in which light and colour are described and quantified, the fundamentals of vision, and the sources of light. These are set out in short chapters, which can be either read as an introduction, skipped by the knowledgeable, or used for reference. The aim is to give a concise description of topics that may make up the lighting syllabus of a degree in architecture, and to include some of the elements of interior design and environmental engineering courses.

The second part, **Designing**, is the main section of the book. It describes the needs and preferences of people in buildings, and shows that there are many criteria of good lighting, ranging from the perceived character and architectural form of a space to the detailed requirements of task performance and comfort. Specific chapters cover design of the overall light and colour of a room, windows, lighting for work and lighting for display. Exterior lighting of buildings is described, and further chapters deal with emergency lighting, energy use and other design constraints.

The third part, **Calculations**, sets out procedures required in practice. Taking some of the most frequently used daylighting and electric lighting calculations, it gives for each a step-by-step synopsis of the method and a realistic worked example. The final chapters list typical data and sources of further information.

A feature of the text is a sequence of tables based on current design codes and data, summarizing good practice and providing checklists. *The Design of Lighting* is planned to be used in conjunction with national standards and codes of practice, giving the designer some of the ideas that lie behind current recommendations, particularly where these have developed out of research in the last ten years.

But underlying all is the belief that lighting is a visual art, no more to be understood from textbooks or accomplished by calculation than any other aspect of architectural design. Learning is primarily by doing – by designing buildings in brightness and colour, by observing and recording. The aim of the whole book is to provide a framework for this.

Acknowledgements

The authors gratefully acknowledge the following sources:

Concord Sylvania, Figures 7.9, 7.10, 8.2, 11.3, 11.4, 12.1, 12.2, 12.6
Judith Torrington, Figure 9.7
Peter Blundell Jones, Figure 7.2
Philips Lighting, Figures 7.5, 12.4, cover photograph
Peter Lathey, Figures 9.3, 9.5
The National Gallery, London, Figures 6.1, 7.3, 7.8, 7.13

Much of the information given in the book is based on printed sources. In particular, the guideline tables of criteria and design recommendations are largely derived from data in publications from the Commission Internationale de l'Eclairage and the Chartered Institution of Building Services Engineers. Several figures, particularly in Part One, draw heavily on widely reproduced illustrations in standard texts on vision and on lighting technology.

The authors also acknowledge help and advice from colleagues at the University of Sheffield, at University College London, and at the Building Research Establishment. They are grateful to their families and to friends in research and in the lighting industry throughout the world for help and encouragement.

Part One

The Technical Background

This is an outline of the physical ideas underlying lighting design. It shows how light and colour can be described, how the human eye responds, how light is produced electrically, and how the light from the sky can be predicted.

It is set out in short chapters, which can be read as an introduction or used for reference.

Describing light

Light is a flow of energy. Like radiant heat, radio waves and X-rays, it is part of the electromagnetic spectrum, and can be described in terms of wavelength and power. But what we see as light can be mixed from many colours, and there is no one-to-one link between the spectral distribution of radiation and human perception of brightness and hue.

For this reason, light is defined uniquely by the response of the human eye. It has its own set of units, which allow it to be quantified, and which are linked to other units of power (such as watts) only by a standardized mathematical description of visual sensitivity.

There are four interrelated units. These describe the flow of light, its intensity in space, illuminance at a point, and the luminance of a surface.

FLOW AND INTENSITY

The first unit of light is the **lumen** (lm). It describes **luminous flux**, the total flow of light from a source, just as the flow of heat from a radiator can be described in watts (W). The output from a lamp is given in lumens. For example:

100 W incandescent lamp	1360 lm
58 W fluorescent tube	5200 lm
400 W high-pressure sodium lamp	48 000 lm

These are typical values, but light output depends on the details of a lamp's construction, and it decreases as the lamp ages.

The relationship between a lamp's light output and its electrical input is known as **luminous efficacy**, measured in lumens per watt. This depends on the physical efficiency of the lamp and the spectral distribution of its output. An incandescent lamp has a low efficacy because most of its power is radiated as heat, in the infrared part of the spectrum, not as light. Efficacies of the three examples are

100 W incandescent lamp	13.6 lm/W
58 W fluorescent tube	90 lm/W
400 W high-pressure sodium lamp	120 lm/W

The performance of a **luminaire** (a light fitting) depends not only on the total amount of light emitted but also on how this is distributed. It could be concentrated in a narrow beam or diffused broadly. The term **luminous intensity** (or just **intensity**) is used to describe the flow of light in a given direction. Intensity is measured in **candelas** (cd). It is calculated from the number of lumens divided by the angular size of the beam, measured in **steradians**: a candela is 1 lumen per steradian. A spotlight used in the home to illuminate a picture might have a luminous intensity of 3000 cd along the axis of its beam.

A **steradian** describes a solid angle, the spatial equivalent of the radian. One steradian is the solid angle at which the area on the surface of a sphere is equal to the radius squared (as shown in Figure 1.1). It is a ratio, and its use in the definition of the candela simplifies calculations.

Figure 1.1 *Solid angle ω. Its size is A/d² steradians.*

ILLUMINANCE AND LUMINANCE

Illuminance, measured in **lux** (lx), is the amount of light falling on a surface (luminous flux density). One lux is given by one lumen falling evenly on a square metre. Here are some typical values of illuminance:

from a candle 1 m away	1 lx
on desks in a general office	500 lx
on the ground from an overcast sky	10 000 lx
from the sun and bright sky in summer	100 000 lx

Standards for lighting are most frequently given as the required lux on the working plane, where the working plane is taken to be a horizontal surface at task level across the room.

The apparent brightness of a surface depends partly on the adaptation state of the eye (which is described in Chapter 3), and partly on the quantity of light reaching the eye from the surface. The term **luminance** (objective brightness) is used to define the physical quantity. The magnitude of the luminance depends on two things: the intensity of light from the surface in the direction of the viewer, and the projected area of the surface emitting or reflecting this light. The smaller the surface area, the brighter it must be to produce a given intensity.

The unit of luminance is therefore the **candela per square metre**. Typical values are:

white paper on an office desk   130 cd/m²
overcast sky   3000 cd/m²
white paper in strong sunlight   25 000 cd/m²

Sky luminance is usually given in cd/m² even though a square metre of sky cannot be visualized.

ALL THE UNITS ARE RELATED

The units are linked together by measures of solid angle and area, as shown in Table 1.1.

Table 1.1   *The units of lighting*

Quantity	Symbol	Unit
Luminous flux	F	lumen (lm)
Luminous intensity: flux/solid angle	I	candela (cd)
Illuminance: flux/area	E	lux (lx)
Luminance: intensity/projected area	L	candela per square metre (cd/m²)

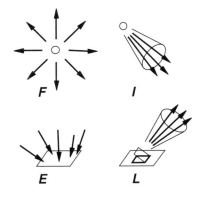

Two basic equations derived from this interrelationship form the foundation for nearly all lighting calculations. The first, which is illustrated in Figure 1.2, gives illuminance in terms of luminous flux and receiving surface area:

A surface in a room receives a fraction, p, of all the light emitted from the lamps in the room. The flux from the lamps is F lumens; the working plane area is A square metres. Then the average illuminance in lux on the surface is

$$E = p\frac{F}{A}$$ (1.1)

This is the basis of the lumen method, which is described in detail in Chapter 16, Example (d). In practice the fraction p is usually taken

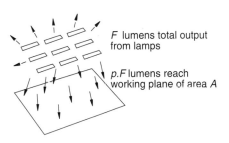

F lumens total output from lamps

p.F lumens reach working plane of area A

Figure 1.2   *Basis of the lumen method calculation.*

to have two components: a **utilization factor**, which takes into account the directionality and reflection of light within the space; and a **maintenance factor**, which indicates reduction of illumination during the lifetime of the lighting installation.

If a source of light is very small, effectively a point in space, the illuminance that it produces on a surface depends on intensity, distance and angle of incidence. This is the second basic equation:

*The intensity of the light in a particular direction from the source is I candelas; the light travels a distance d metres and falls on a surface at an angle θ (this angle of incidence is measured between the direction of light and the **normal**, or **perpendicular**, to the surface). The illuminance on the surface is, in lux,*

$$E = \frac{I \cos\theta}{d^2} \tag{1.2}$$

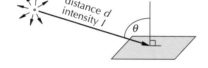

Figure 1.3   *Illuminance from a point source.*

This equation embodies the inverse square law and Lambert's law (which says that the amount of light falling on a surface is proportional to the cosine of the angle of incidence). See Figure 1.3.

No real lamp is a point source, but the equation can be used with negligible error when the dimensions of the source are small in relation to the distance d (a maximum source size of $d/5$ is often taken to be the limit) and when the rays are not focused by an optical system. Chapter 16 shows how the equation is used to calculate illuminance from sources such as spotlights.

REFLECTION AND TRANSMISSION

The fraction of the incident light that is reflected back by a surface is the **reflectance**, denoted by the Greek letter rho (ρ). Reflectance is a value between zero and one: $\rho = 0$ if the surface is perfect black and therefore absorbs all light; $\rho = 1$ if all incident light is reflected.

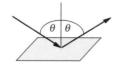

Figure 1.4   *Specular reflection.*

The direction of the reflected beam depends on the nature of the surface. A **specular reflector** is a mirror: a ray is reflected in the same plane as the incident ray and at an angle equal to the angle of incidence, as in Figure 1.4. The luminance of a perfectly specular surface does not depend on its illuminance but on the luminance of the objects seen reflected. A **diffuse reflector** is a matt surface that scatters light evenly in all directions. The luminance of a perfect diffuser is proportional to its illuminance, and is the same from every angle of view.

No real surface is either entirely specular or diffusing. Sometimes it is useful to give two reflectances for a material, specular and diffuse; and for scientific study a directional reflectance function may be necessary, specifying how a beam of light at any incident angle is scattered. For lighting calculations in buildings it is usually enough to assume that diffuse reflection is dominant and that a single value of ρ for a particular material describes its total reflectance. Typical reflectances are:

white paper	0.8
clean concrete	0.4
dark wood	0.1

With a diffuse reflector, as in Figure 1.5, luminance (cd/m²) is directly proportional to illuminance and reflectance:

$$L = \frac{E\rho}{\pi} \tag{1.3}$$

The link between luminance, area and intensity, as in Figure 1.6, completes the chain:

If the area of a patch of surface is A m², its luminance is L cd/m², and it is facing an angle ϕ away from the line of sight, then the intensity towards the viewer is

$$I = LA\cos\phi \tag{1.4}$$

For this intensity to be used to calculate the illuminance on another surface with equation (1.2), the size of the bright patch must be small in relation to the distance. This may mean that the patch must be subdivided into small zones and the calculation repeated for each of them. Alternatively, for advanced calculations there are formulae that give directly the illuminance from line and area sources.

Transmittance is the fraction of light that passes through a material. It also is a number between zero and one, and is denoted by the Greek letter tau (τ). Sometimes it is useful to specify **diffuse transmittance**, the fraction of a beam that is uniformly scattered, and **regular transmittance**, the fraction that remains as a geometrical ray.

In all real transparent materials there is some reflection at surfaces, some absorption and some scattering. The sum of the total reflectance and the total transmittance must be a number between zero and one. With a material such as glass, the fractions that are reflected and transmitted depend on the angle of incidence. When a beam strikes a glass surface at a glancing angle it is mainly reflected; when it is perpendicular to the surface most of it passes through. For simple calculations of window performance an average transmittance

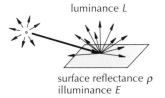

luminance L

surface reflectance ρ
illuminance E

Figure 1.5 *Luminance of a diffuse reflector.*

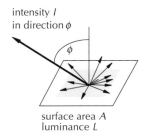

intensity I
in direction ϕ

ϕ

surface area A
luminance L

Figure 1.6 *Intensity and luminance.*

is used, a weighted mean over all directions of incidence. Typical values of daylight transmittance are:

clear 6 mm sheet glass without dirt   0.8
clear double glazing with average dirt   0.5

The transmittance of glass to light differs from its transmittance of total solar radiation or of radiant heat because the transparency of the material varies with wavelength. Separate values are used for daylighting and solar gain calculations. But all absorbed energy, whatever the wavelength of the incident radiation, increases the temperature of a material. All the light that enters a room is ultimately absorbed by surfaces and is therefore a thermal gain.

Chapter 16 gives typical reflectances of building materials and some examples of glazing transmittance.

Describing colour

2

It is not enough for a designer to describe a colour just as 'red', or even 'strong yellowish red': colour names have different meanings to different people. To match colours accurately or to achieve subtle mixtures requires a far more precise method of specification.

But practicality is not the only reason for developing a conceptual structure of colour. Having a framework for visualizing chromatic relationships can be creatively helpful: for instance, the sequence given in Chapter 8 for selecting colours is based on a concept of colour classification.

SURFACE COLOURS

The simplest method of ensuring standardization is to have a reference set of actual colour samples. A manufacturer's card of paint colours or a swatch of fabric samples lets the consumer make an unambiguous choice: all that is necessary is to quote the number or name by which the item is labelled.

Such a set of samples is called a **colour atlas**. Its use is not, however, foolproof. In any colour manufacturing or printing process there is variation from one batch to another, so different copies of a reference set are never exactly identical. But, more importantly, the appearance of pigments depends on the nature of the light falling on them. Two surface colours can appear similar under one illuminant and significantly different under another (a phenomenon known as **metamerism**). A colour atlas must always be viewed under the same type of illumination, and this is normally assumed to be light of a continuous spectrum such as daylight.

But an atlas consisting of only a set of samples cannot itself provide exact specification of intermediate colours. The solution is to create axes along which individual points are set, just as longitude and latitude can be used to specify a place on a globe. Colour, though, requires three dimensions.

These three dimensions are most commonly called **hue**, **value** and **chroma**. Hue is a point on the colour circle, value varies with the reflectance of the coloured surface, and chroma varies with the saturation of the colour. The dimensions can be visualized when a strong pigment is added to a neutral grey paint. The hue is given by the pigment, the chroma by the amount of pigment added, and the value by the neutral paint that would have the same reflectance as the final mixture.

The terms hue, value and chroma are those of the Munsell system, first published in 1905 by A.H. Munsell, a Boston art teacher. In this system, the hue circle is divided into ten main segments: red, yellow-red, round to purple and red-purple, as in Figure 2.1. Each segment is further divided into ten divisions around the pure hue. The hue is then coded: 5Y, for example, is pure yellow.

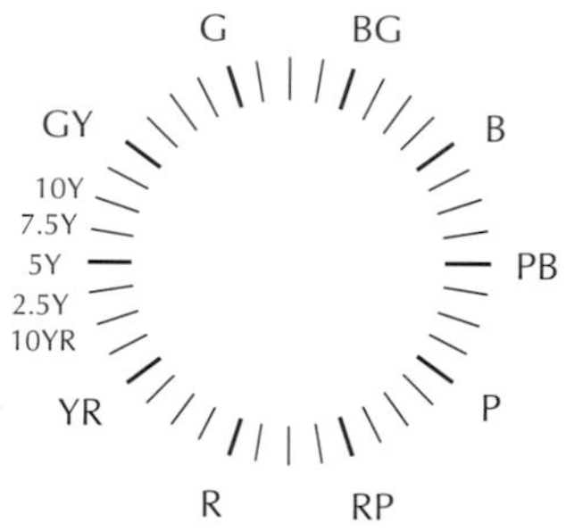

The hue circle can be made into a colour disc by placing a grey point in the centre and increasing saturation radially from this neutral to the pure hue. The distance from the centre is Munsell's indicator of chroma: zero indicates neutral, a high number an intensely saturated colour.

Value is the third dimension. Black has a value equal to zero, white a value of 10. The reflectance of a coloured surface is given approximately by a simple function of the Munsell value:

$$\rho \approx \frac{\text{value}\,(\text{value}-1)}{100} \tag{2.1}$$

Figure 2.1 *The Munsell hue circle.*

The dimensions can be visualized as a colour solid, as in Figure 2.2.

Each point within the Munsell solid is a unique colour and has a complete reference in the form

hue   value / chroma

except for neutrals, which are denoted by N, with only value.

For example:

light yellow	5Y 8/0.5
deep red-purple	7.5 RP 2/4
dark grey	N 3

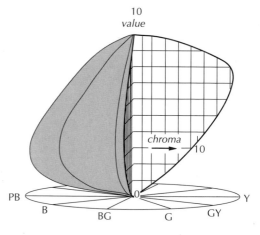

Figure 2.2 *The Munsell colour solid, cut to show scales of value and chroma across a hue.*

Within each dimension equal increments are intended to indicate equal steps in perceived contrast, although the spacing varies between dimensions. The solid is asymmetrical because the values of apparently fully saturated hues differ: a strong yellow paint looks lighter and has a higher reflectance than a saturated blue.

The colour solid can be imagined as a fruit, with the core white at the top and black at the base, and the skin graduated to give a surface of spectral colours. Unlike an apple, the inside also is coloured and graduated: a worm burrowing across in a straight line might begin eating yellow, pass through mid-grey, and emerge from dark blue.

The **Natural Colour System** is an alternative method of defining surface colours. In this system, a colour is defined by its position within a set of six elementary colours: white and black, plus the **chromatic elements** yellow, red, blue and green. The chromatic elements are set at the quarter points of a colour circle, and an intermediate hue is given as a percentage of the distance along the arc between each adjacent pair. An orange, halfway between yellow and red, is denoted Y50R, while a red with only a tinge of yellow is Y90R. The circle of chromatic colours is shown in Figure 2.3.

A colour that is not fully saturated is denoted by its position in a triangle formed between white, black and a chromatic colour. The edges of the triangle form the axes of whiteness, blackness and chromaticness. The colour solid is thus a double cone, as in Figure 2.4. The top point is white, the base point is black and the colour circle forms the rim.

The sum of blackness, whiteness and chromaticness at any point equals 100%. In notation blackness and chromaticness are given two digits each while whiteness is omitted because it is a redundant dimension. The format used is

blackness chromaticness – hue

Deep red-purple could be described by 7315 – R24B. That is, 73% blackness, 15% chromaticness, with a hue 24% of the distance along the arc between red and blue in the colour circle.

The NCS equivalents of the other Munsell examples are

dark grey   7501 – R97B
light yellow   2002 – Y03R

Unlike the Munsell system there is no simple relationship between equal increments along the dimensions and equal steps in perceived colour difference, nor is there an approximate link to reflectance.

Within the UK a system for specifying surface colour is given in British Standard BS 5252. This is an atlas of 237 colours on a reference system that uses the three dimensions of hue, greyness and weight. The first of these is comparable with Munsell hue, while greyness is comparable with chroma except in the designation of white and black. Weight, though, is based on subjective lightness instead of reflectance, and therefore does not correlate well with value because colours of the same reflectance in different saturated hues do not appear equally light.

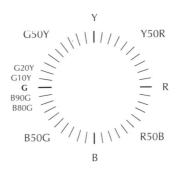

Figure 2.3 *The NCS hue circle.*

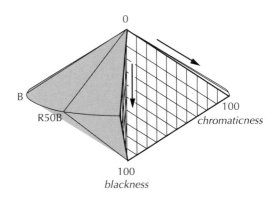

Figure 2.4 *The NCS colour solid, cut to show scales of blackness and chromaticness.*

Hues, in the BS notation, are designated by a two-digit even number: 00 represents neutral, 02 red-purple, 04 red, and then in steps round the colour circles to 24 purple. Greyness is given by a letter from A (grey) to E (clear or pure hue). Weight is given by a two-digit odd number, 01 indicating a very low weight.

The system was intended to help designers to select colour combinations, but it has not received widespread support.

The format of BS 5252 notation is

hue   greyness   weight

and the examples become

dark grey	00 A 13
light yellow	10 A 03
deep red-purple	02 C 40

COLOURED LIGHTS AND CHROMATICITY

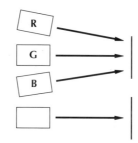

Figure 2.5 *Matching lights: additive colour.*

If, as in Figure 2.5, three different coloured lamps are focused to shine together onto a white surface, the resulting mixture of light can be changed in colour by altering the relative outputs of the sources. It might be possible to adjust the combination so that the patch of light from a fourth, different, lamp appears identical in colour.

To be able to match a broad range of other colours, the source lamps, the **primaries**, must be strongly saturated and be widely spaced in hue around the colour circle (red, green and blue, for example). Then, if the primaries are standardized, another colour could be defined by the combination that gives the same appearance. It could be written

r of Red + g of Green + b of Blue

If these are expressed in relative quantities so that $r + g + b = 1$, the mixture can be plotted as a point in a triangle, as Figure 2.6.

The superimposition of lights gives **additive** colour mixing: an apparently white light can be obtained by combining the primaries. (**Subtractive** colour mixing occurs when paints are mixed: a combination of red, blue and green pigments approaches black because each colour absorbs part of the total incident light. Subtractive mixing occurs also when light-transmitting materials such as filters are combined.)

But not every colour can be matched by a set of three primaries. Those excluded are other saturated spectral sources. A combination of light from red and green lamps produces yellow, but a more intense colour can be obtained from a pure yellow source. A matching combination could occur only if the pure yellow were desaturated with some light from the blue primary – so in the *rgb* specification the blue component would take a negative value.

The **CIE chromaticity diagram** (Figure 2.6) is based on three imaginary sources with standardized spectral distributions such that any real colour can be matched by some combination of these primaries. The full spectrum now follows the curved line in the diagram, and a triangle of colours matched by three actual lamps lies inside this. A mathematical transformation is used to plot test results onto the graph.

The *y* axis indicates greenness, on a scale 0–1; the *x* axis indicates redness; and, because the sum of the three primaries is unity, the value of $1 - x - y$ indicates blueness. Neutral colours lie close to the centre of the triangle.

Any colour of light, or a surface under a particular illuminant, or a TV screen phosphor, can be represented graphically by a point on the diagram, or numerically by the *x* and *y* coordinates. Mixtures can be predicted: the colours of all combinations of two coloured lights lie on a straight line between the graph points of the lights.

Several derivations of the original 1931 CIE diagram have been advanced. These include the *u, v* and *u′, v′* forms, which aim to improve the perceptual uniformity so that a distance on the diagram represents a similar perceptual difference in every colour.

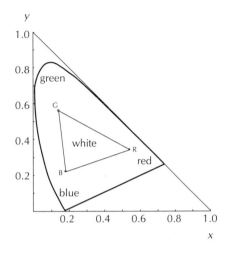

Figure 2.6 *The CIE x,y chromaticity diagram. The triangle formed by plotting the coordinates of three actual lamp colours shows the range of colours that can be matched by mixing these.*

Seeing light and colour

3

The eye is not a camera. Although optical images are focused onto a light-sensitive surface at the back of the eye, these images are not what we perceive. In a series of transformations carried out first in the retina itself (the light-sensitive cells) and then in stages through to the visual cortex of the brain, the information is changed: the balance of brightness and colour is altered; attention is concentrated on small zones while large areas are unnoticed; images of the present scene are replaced by earlier images from memory. What we 'see' depends on experience and on what we have learnt, as well as on the physical structure of eye and brain.

But the physical system itself has many characteristics relevant to lighting design. They determine such factors as the range of brightness that can be perceived with comfort, sensitivity to visual changes, and the way coloured surfaces are recognized. This chapter introduces some concepts of vision that are used later in the book, especially in Chapter 9 on task lighting.

ADAPTATION

The eye alters in sensitivity in response to the light falling on it. This change can be seen when the pupil gets smaller in bright light, although contraction of the iris is not the main mechanism of adaptation but a fine adjustment for greater depth of field. The pupil changes in area over a range of about 16 to 1, but the eye is sensitive over a range of several million to one. It is the photoreceptors themselves, the light-sensitive cells of the retina, that make the adaptation. They contain pigments that are broken down by photons, releasing electrical energy and becoming less sensitive in the process. Once the light is removed, the pigments gradually regenerate so that sensitivity is regained. It is a process of

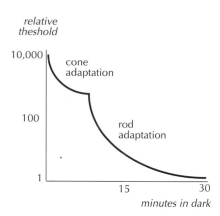

relative theshold

Figure 3.1 *Adaptation to darkness.*

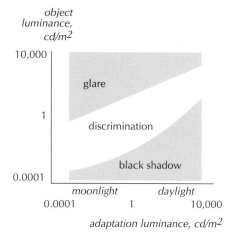

object luminance, cd/m²

Figure 3.2 *Range of luminance discrimination.*

self-regulation: the retina adapts itself to optimum sensitivity for the ambient lighting.

The bleaching out process is fast – a few seconds – while complete regeneration can take as long as an hour. Switching on the light when waking up at night gives only a short time of blinding glare; but it is many minutes before details of a dark room, such as a cinema, can be perceived after entering it from daylight. Figure 3.1 shows the time scale of dark adaptation. The step in the curve occurs because there are two types of photoreceptor in the retina, known as **rods** and **cones**. The rods are sensitive at low levels of light but are bleached out at the daytime levels, and can take 30 minutes to become fully dark-adapted; also, they do not give recognition of colour. The cones are sensitive only at brighter levels; three types of cone in the retina respond to different wavelengths and are the basis of colour vision.

Figure 3.2 illustrates how at every level of adaptation there is a limited range of brightness discrimination. Above this range, areas of very high luminance are glaring; within the central range the eye can sensitively distinguish between surfaces that differ only slightly in luminance; but below this all areas seem black, and little discrimination is possible. At the adaptation levels corresponding with normal room lighting the range of discrimination from the upper to the lower limit is about 1000 : 1. Brightness adaptation affects our ability to see small detail and small differences in contrast, and thus how we perform visual tasks. This is described in Chapter 9.

There is also visual adaptation to colour, especially the colour of ambient lighting: a surface appears to maintain the same hue when seen in light of gradually changing colour. We rarely recognize a change in room colours when daylight slowly varies, even though the colour of skylight can change greatly during the course of a morning. More complex types of visual adaptation, such as to tilt and to motion, also occur in everyday activities. For example, immediately after travelling in a car at high speed, movement at moderate speeds can seem very slow.

CENTRAL AND PERIPHERAL VISION

The alert eye is continuously in motion, and adjusts itself so that any object of interest is held within a central field of view about 2° across. This is about the height of a line of print in a book held a normal reading distance away. The ability to discern small detail – **visual acuity** – is greatest in this zone, and reduces by 50% only 5° from the centre. The small area of the retina in the central focus is called the **fovea**, and the central visual field is **foveal vision**.

Peripheral vision is especially sensitive to motion. Probably a relic of survival needs, there is automatic awareness of objects coming into the field of vision, a continuing monitoring of the ground when walking. Sudden changes of brightness, such as flashing lights, are noticed more when they occur at the edge of the visual field.

Foveal and peripheral vision are different and complementary. Having central vision alone is like being in a dark and unfamiliar room with a narrow-beamed torch: it is possible to scan about and pick up fine detail, yet be uncertain of the surroundings. To have peripheral vision alone is like entering a strange room that is dimly lit: the whole space can be perceived, but not in detail.

Colour and brightness sensitivities vary across the retina. The fovea comprises cone cells alone, and is therefore insensitive at low levels of light. Rods dominate the peripheral field, so colour is perceived poorly there. Movement of the eyes normally masks this partial insensitivity to colour, but if the gaze is fixed ahead and a coloured card is brought gradually into the field of view, the observer is aware of the moving object before the colour can be recognized.

WAVELENGTH, BRIGHTNESS AND COLOUR

When sunlight is split into a spectrum – as in a rainbow – the colours do not appear equally strong. The central bands of yellow and green have a much higher apparent brightness than the orange-red at one extreme or the purple-blue at the other. This is due primarily to the eye's varying sensitivity, and it reflects the definition of light as human perception of radiation.

Figure 3.3 shows how the eye gives its maximum response to colours in the centre of the spectrum. Ultraviolet radiation, beyond the left of the curve, is not perceived by the eye: it is not 'light'. A beam of radiation of constant power but gradually increasing wavelength would first look dull purple, and then a stronger blue, a bright green, a fading and reddening orange and dull crimson before finally becoming invisible again as the beam reached infrared.

The graph is the V_λ **curve**, the average visual response of the human eye in a light-adapted state. A similar function describes the average response of the human eye at low illumination, but this curve is shifted slightly to the left. Blue light, to the dark-adapted eye, is relatively brighter than red, but at the lowest brightnesses neither is perceived as a hue.

The relationship between the eye's sensitivity and the spectral distribution of radiation, quantified by the V_λ curve, determines the luminous efficacy of a source. If all the electric power entering a

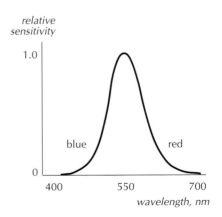

Figure 3.3 *Sensitivity to spectral colour of the light-adapted eye: the V_λ curve.*

lamp could be converted to radiation at the eye's peak sensitivity, the luminous efficacy would be 683 lm/W. A lamp that has an output totally in the yellow-green region gives more light for the same radiated power than one giving a full spectrum. There is therefore opposition between the luminous efficacy of a light source and its colour-rendering capabilities: to achieve a high efficacy not only should a lamp be designed to minimize power dissipated as conducted or radiated heat, or as radiation in the ultraviolet, but its visible output should be concentrated in the yellow-green. But for good colour rendering the lamp should have a balanced and continuous spectral output, which includes the colour extremes where the eye responds weakly. Chapter 4 describes this in more detail.

MIXTURES AND CONSTANCY

When several notes are played together on the piano, a chord is heard, not a single intermediate tone. With musical training the component notes can be identified and reproduced; the intervals between them even have names such as octave, fifth and minor third.

The ability to hear the component notes of a chord is not reflected in sight. Human vision is unable to separate the constituent wavelengths of a light source spectrum. For example, a mixture of red and green light falling on a white surface can be made to look the same yellow as the light of a low-pressure sodium lamp, because the eye cannot perceive the difference in spectral composition. This is of practical importance: paint colours can be mixed, and colour television and colour printing can occur, because of this absence of a one-to-one link between spectral wavelength and perceived hue.

But a different sort of discrimination *can* be made. Although a grey-painted surface and a white surface with lower illuminance may have the same luminance, they normally look different. Provided the light source is not concealed, the eye can separate the effects of surface and illuminant. The terms **lightness** (a term associated with surface reflectance) and **brightness** (which relates to luminance) are often used to distinguish this difference.

The word **constancy** is used to describe recognition of an unchanging characteristic when there is objective ambiguity. Size constancy occurs when an object is perceived as moving into the distance rather than shrinking, even though in both cases the same retinal image of the object is produced. Constancy of surface colour occurs when the eye can distinguish a piece of coloured material from white material illuminated by a coloured lamp. For this to happen the brain must be able to infer how the colour is produced.

The phenomenon of constancy indicates the sophistication of the eye and brain in their analysis of images. Clues from the whole visual field and from past experience are used subconsciously to select a visual pattern's most likely interpretation. Perceptual constancy can, though, be overridden by unusual or deliberately illusory scenes, and when this happens the visual field is, literally, confusing.

SOME NON-VISUAL EFFECTS OF LIGHT

The 24-hour pattern of daylight and darkness triggers the human body's cycle of alertness and sleep. An innate circadian rhythm is synchronized with daytime and night-time by a response to high levels of light (typically a few thousand lux) in early morning and late afternoon. The absence of these stimuli can cause poor night-time sleep and difficulties of concentration by day; a high proportion of profoundly blind people report such symptoms. Exposure to periods of bright light can also aid the adjustment of shift workers to new hours, and can ameliorate jet-lag; and, in a related effect, high lighting levels can increase the alertness of workers, both on night shifts and in the afternoon when the body's arousal is beginning its diurnal decline.

An extreme condition of light deprivation is seasonal affective disorder (SAD), a psychiatric depression that can occur in winter among those living in northern cities. The symptoms can be relieved by regular daily exposure to bright light.

Light from electricity

4

The first electric light, a carbon arc, was demonstrated in the middle of the nineteenth century. But it was the development of the incandescent lamp at about the same time by Joseph Swan in Great Britain and by Thomas Edison in the USA that heralded the start of electric lighting as we know it. Electric lamps have improved dramatically in quality, efficiency and convenience since the early times, but new light sources are still being developed.

Primarily there are two types of lamp used in buildings: incandescent and discharge. Each is available in a wide range, with variation in size, power, colour appearance, colour rendering, efficacy and operating characteristics. The lighting designer needs to be familiar with the different lamps available, and this information is best obtained from manufacturers' catalogues.

INCANDESCENT LAMPS – THE HEATED FILAMENT

The incandescent lamp depends on passing an electric current through a wire to such an extent that it glows white hot. Tungsten wire is now used, but early lamps used carbon filaments; it is necessary to have a material with a high melting point so that it emits light for a reasonable length of time without breaking. The tungsten wire is usually coiled and coiled again to produce a fine filament. This is supported on two lead wires, which connect it to the electricity supply.

The bulb usually contains an inert gas to stop the filament oxidizing; sometimes a vacuum is used. But gradually, as the lamp operates, tungsten evaporates from the filament and is deposited on the inside of the bulb. The filament becomes thinner and eventually breaks. An inert gas filling retards this process and ensures a reasonable lamp life, typically about 1000 hours. The actual life varies

relative life

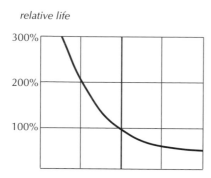

relative light
output

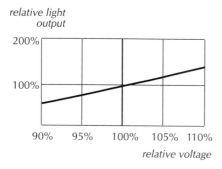

relative voltage

Figure 4.1 *Variation with voltage of the life and light output of an incandescent lamp.*

relative
power

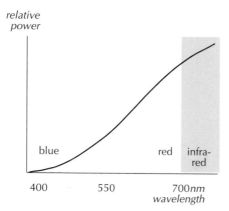

Figure 4.2 *Spectral output of an incandescent lamp.*

within a batch of lamps, and although a mean value can be quoted this may not be helpful. Lamp manufacturers often give the life as the point when they expect a particular percentage of lamps to have failed.

The performance of the lamp is determined primarily by the operating temperature of the filament. As this increases, there are three important consequences: the colour of the light produced becomes whiter; there is an increase in luminous efficacy (the amount of light produced in relation to the energy input); and the life of the lamp is shortened. A small change in the electricity supply voltage therefore has a major effect. This is shown in Figure 4.1. An increase in applied voltage of 5% (for instance, from 240 to 252 V) causes an increase in luminous output of 20%, but the operating life is halved. Conversely, underrunning an incandescent lamp increases life significantly but reduces the light output.

The colour appearance of an incandescent lamp is described by its **colour temperature**, measured in kelvins. This is related to the temperature of the filament. A normal tungsten filament lamp has a colour temperature of about 2800 K – a relatively warm colour appearance. The spectrum of radiant energy from the lamp has the shape shown in Figure 4.2. Its smooth continuity means that its **colour rendering** is good: the light allows fairly accurate discrimination between one surface colour and another. But the output is not uniform across the visible range: there is far more energy in the red than the blue wavelengths. This causes the warm appearance but means also that red surfaces illuminated by the lamp may look brighter than blue surfaces of the same reflectance.

Most of the radiant output – over 90% of it – is not in the visible part of the spectrum; the peak occurs far into the invisible infrared region. The majority of energy from an incandescent lamp is emitted as radiant heat, which is why its luminous efficacy is low, typically 12 lm/W.

A major development of the incandescent lamp followed the discovery of the halogen cycle. In this process the tungsten that evaporates is redeposited back onto the filament. It occurs when a halogen, usually iodine or bromine, is included with the filling, and the gas temperature is controlled. The performance effect of this is an increase of lamp life to typically 2000 hours, an increase in colour appearance to 3000 K, and an increase in efficacy to typically 20 lm/W.

Incandescent lamps are produced in many different bulb shapes and finishes: clear and diffuse, as well as a range of colours. The bulbs can be partly silvered and formed into an integral reflector to make spotlamps. A range of these is available, with various beam shapes and intensities. Small compact tungsten halogen lamps, particularly those operating at low voltage (usually 12 or 24 V), can be used with precise optics to provide accurate light control. A family of very small low-voltage spotlamps is available. Used extensively for display lighting, these lamps are operated on mains voltage with small transformers.

DISCHARGE LAMPS – THE GLOWING GAS

Light can be produced by an electric discharge in a gas-filled transparent tube. The discharge is started by applying a high voltage across the electrodes at each end. This ionizes the gas filling, enabling an increasing current to flow, and resulting in further ionization. The radiation produced depends on the materials in the tube and on the gas pressure. Its spectrum is discontinuous, and comprises bands of radiation at specific wavelengths. Phosphor coatings on the inside wall of the tube may be used to absorb some of the radiation and re-emit it at different wavelengths – especially to convert ultraviolet radiation to energy in the visible range.

With all discharge lamps additional equipment is required in the electrical circuit. This produces an initial high voltage to start the discharge, then limits the current during operation and controls the power factor. The power factor depends on the relationship between voltage and current in an a.c. circuit, and affects the efficiency of the equipment. The combined efficacy of a lamp and its control circuit determine the energy efficiency.

The colour appearance of a discharge lamp is specified by the **correlated colour temperature** (CCT): the temperature in kelvins of the black-body radiation that appears closest to the colour appearance of light from the lamp. A colour temperature below 3300 K is often describes as **warm**, between 3300 and 5300 K as **intermediate**, and over 5300 K as **cold**.

The **CIE general colour rendering index** (R_a) provides a measure of a lamp's colour rendering quality around the hue circle, quantified on a scale from 0 to 100. Because it has a continuous spectrum the incandescent lamp is used as a reference, and is assigned $R_a = 100$. Lamps with an R_a greater than 90 are considered to be very good, and are used where accurate colour matching or discrimination is required. Those with an R_a in the range 80–89 are appropriate where accurate colour judgement is necessary or where good colour judgement is required for reasons of appearance. Lamps with an R_a below 80 should be used only where colour quality is of little importance.

The most commonly used discharge lamp is the **low-pressure fluorescent tube**. This uses primarily a mercury discharge, which emits a large part of its energy as ultraviolet radiation. The inside wall of the lamp tube is lined with a phosphor powder, which absorbs the ultraviolet and re-radiates the energy in the visible spectrum.

Since its introduction in the early 1940s the lamp has gone through many developments. Much work has been done on phosphor compositions, and now it is possible to have lamps with colour appearances ranging from warm to cold. The lamp is efficient, with a high efficacy, although the actual value depends on the phosphor composition. Typically, a modern fluorescent lamp using multi-phosphor technology with good colour rendering ($R_a = 80$) has an efficacy of 80–100 lm/W. The life is usually 8000–10 000 hours, but the light output reduces gradually with age.

Originally the electrical circuit for fluorescent lamps included a wire-wound inductive ballast, a starter switch and a power factor capacitor. Recently, electronic circuits have been introduced. These operate lamps at very high frequencies, 20–30 kHz rather than the 50 Hz of the normal mains supply. The very high frequency improves energy efficiency, but comfort is also improved because lamp flicker is undetectable. A further advantage of electronic circuits is the ability to regulate or to dim the light output. The light from the lamp can be controlled to vary with daylight or dimmed for special conditions.

The fluorescent tube has near instant switch-on and restrike, especially with electronic control. The light output increases from switch-on, usually reaching its maximum after a few minutes, but the change in output after switch-on will be hardly noticed.

The output of a fluorescent lamp depends on the temperature of the coolest spot on the bulb wall and therefore on the ambient temperature. If a fluorescent lamp is to be used at low ambient temperatures (in a cold store, for example) or at high ambient temperatures (such as in a bakery) then the lamp light output will be different in the two extremes from normal operating temperatures.

In the **compact fluorescent lamp** (or CFL) the lamp tube is folded and combined with an integral control circuit to form a discharge lamp with a volume similar to that occupied by an equivalent incandescent lamp. The early versions, developed during the 1980s, were heavy because of the integral control gear, but they formed an important breakthrough in lamp development. There has since been considerable improvement, and now it is possible to have CFLs with either integral or separate control gear. It is likely that this type will become one of the most commonly used lamps, and a direct replacement of incandescent lamps for many purposes.

Compact fluorescent lamps have good colour-rendering properties and come in a range of different colour appearances. Lamp life is high, typically 8000–10 000 hours, but the output decreases with age. Efficacy is typically 50–70 lm/W: this is high by comparison with incandescent lamps but less than that of the tubular fluorescent.

Cold-cathode lamps have an unheated filament but require high-voltage control gear. They have long, thin tubes, which can be bent into signs or shaped to fit architectural features. Their life is long, 30 000 hours, but their efficacy is typically about 50 lm/W. When filled with gases other than mercury vapour, and the phosphor coating omitted, they can produce light in various colours.

The **high-pressure discharge lamp** has a small discharge tube contained within a tubular or elliptical outer bulb; there is not necessarily a fluorescent coating. It is much smaller than the tubular fluorescent lamp but operates similarly; it also requires ancillary electrical control equipment to initiate the discharge, control the current, and correct the power factor. A high-pressure discharge lamp takes a few minutes to achieve full light output; if switched off and back on again, there is a delay before the lamp cools sufficiently for the arc to form again, unless hot restrike control gear is provided.

The **high-pressure mercury lamp** was the first to be introduced, in the 1930s. It was used almost exclusively for street lighting, because although it was efficient compared with incandescent sources it had a very poor colour appearance and rendering. The lamp comprises a quartz arc tube contained within either an elliptical or a reflector-shaped outer bulb. It has long life, typically 10 000 hours, and a reasonable efficacy, 40–60 lm/W. In the lamp's basic form the colour performance is poor, but this is significantly improved in versions of the lamp with phosphor coating inside the bulb.

In the 1960s a development of the mercury high-pressure discharge lamp occurred that raised its colour quality to the point where it could be used where colour rendering and appearance were important. In the **metal halide lamp**, halogens are added to the mercury vapour. To do this successfully requires advanced manufacturing technology. Initially the colour appearance of some lamps tended to change through life: this was particularly noticeable when several were used in the same installation and could be easily compared, but the technology has been developed intensively and the major lamp makers have minimized this effect.

The lamp comes in a range of shapes and sizes, including versions with integral reflectors. Some lamps have very small arc tubes, which makes them ideal for precise optical control luminaires, such as spotlights for sports lighting. The lamp life is typically 8000–10 000 hours with an efficacy of 70–100 lm/W. In addition to the 'white' metal halide lamp, coloured lamps, particularly blue and green, are produced by some manufacturers for decorative purposes.

The other main group of lamps is based on a discharge through sodium vapour. The **low-pressure sodium lamp** has a bright orange monochromatic light. It is used only where colour is unimportant and high efficacy is required; motorway lighting is the major application. The low-pressure sodium lamp is available in a range of sizes, all with tubular bulb shapes. Typically it has a life of 8000–10 000 hours and an efficacy of 100–200 lm/W.

Lamp scientists had known for some time that if a sodium discharge at high pressure could be created, a much improved colour performance could be achieved. As the pressure of a sodium discharge is raised, the spectrum of monochromatic radiation at low pressure expands to produce a broadband distribution. The problem was to find a light-transmitting material that could contain the highly corrosive sodium at high pressure. In the 1960s a translucent ceramic material, sintered alumina, was developed. Research has continued on this, making possible further increases in arc pressure and hence even better colour performance. Currently the high-pressure sodium lamp is available in a range of sizes and bulb shapes. The best colour versions are described as 'White SON'. The lamp has a long life, typically 8000–10 000 hours, with an efficacy of 70–120 lm/W.

The development of lamps is a continuing process, and two new types of lamp have been recently introduced. The **mercury induction lamp** depends on energizing a mercury discharge using a magnetic field. Because this eliminates the need for electrodes, which deteriorate with time, the lamp life can be extremely long: typically 60 000 hours is quoted by the manufacturers. The lamp is basically a fluorescent tube and has a similar colour quality, with an efficacy of approximately 60 lm/W.

The **sulphur microwave lamp** is an electrodeless source, which uses microwaves to create light from a sulphur and argon bulb filling. The prototypes produce 450 000 lm for an energy consumption of 5.9 kW: an efficacy of approximately 76 lm/W. The life is estimated to be 10 000 hours, based on the life of the magnetron that generates the microwaves. The spectral distribution is continuous across the whole spectrum range, with reasonable colour performance. With a source of this power a system is necessary to distribute the light within buildings; the sulphur lamp cannot be used as direct replacement for existing sources until small sizes can be manufactured. A 1 kW version is commercially available.

WHICH LAMP?

Table 4.1 lists the characteristics of some incandescent and discharge lamps. Each type of lamp is produced in many versions, varying in power, efficacy and colour, so it is necessary to use manufacturers' data when designing. The values in the table given for efficacy are those for a lamp plus its control equipment (if any); the design life is a relative value, taking into account the probability of failure and long-term reduction in light output.

Table 4.1 *Typical lamp characteristics*

There is a wide range of lamps available in each group, varying in characteristics. Manufacturer's data must be used when specifying particular lamps.

Standard incandescent

Circuit luminous efficacy	12 lm/W
Design life	1000 hours
Colour	R_a 100, 2800 K
Control gear required?	No

Tungsten halogen

Circuit luminous efficacy	20 lm/W
Design life	2000 hours
Colour	R_a 100, 3000 K
Control gear required?	Transformer (for low voltages)

Tubular fluorescent

Circuit luminous efficacy	80 lm/W
Design life	8000 hours
Colour	R_a 85, 2700–6500 K
Control gear required?	Yes

Compact fluorescent

Circuit luminous efficacy	60 lm/W
Design life	8000 hours
Colour	R_a 80, 2700–4000 K
Control gear required?	Yes

High-pressure mercury fluorescent

Circuit luminous efficacy	50 lm/W
Design life	10 000 hours
Colour	R_a 60, 3300 K
Control gear required?	Yes

Metal halide

Circuit luminous efficacy	80 lm/W
Design life	8000 hours
Colour	R_a 80, 4000 K
Control gear required?	Yes

High-pressure sodium

Circuit luminous efficacy	90 lm/W
Design life	12 000 hours
Colour	R_a 60, 2400 K
Control gear required?	Yes

Choosing a lamp for a particular application means that a balance has to be made between different requirements. Table 4.2 lists some of the points to be considered.

Table 4.2 *Short checklist for choosing a lamp*

Power and output
Power rating (watts), light output (lumens) and efficacy (lumens/watt)

Dimensions and durability
Bulb size and shape, burning position, mechanical strength

Colour
Colour rendering index (R_a) and colour appearance (correlated colour temperature, K)

Lifetime
Lamp life (hours) and lumen depreciation

Control
Type of control gear required, lamp run-up time (minutes), restrike performance and ability to dim

Thermal
Lamp envelope temperature, lamp operation with respect to ambient temperature

CONTROLLING THE LIGHT

A luminaire has several functions. It must give the lamp physical support and protection; it must enclose electrical connections; it must support any associated control gear; it must have an appearance that is architecturally appropriate. Above all it has to provide optical control so that the light output has the required distribution.

Several techniques for redirecting light are available to the luminaire designer, and include the following:

- **Obstruction.** This is the use of masks to control the light. An example is the provision of louvres to limit discomfort glare caused by a view of bare lamps. Another example is the simple drum fitting, which obstructs light to the sides but allows light to travel both up and down. Elements of a building (such as coves, cornices and pelmets) can be used to provide obstruction, integrating the luminaire with the building itself.

- **Reflection.** A flat mirror redirects a ray of light so that the angles of incidence and reflection are the same, relative to the normal of the mirror. If the reflector is curved, the rays from the source can be focused. A non-specular surface scatters light; if the surface is perfectly diffusing, or 'matt', it scatters light evenly in all directions, so the luminance of the surface is constant from all directions of view. Together, the shape of the surface, its specularity and its reflectance can be used to determine the luminaire's beam shape. Spotlights used in buildings depend primarily on a focused reflection.

- **Refraction.** The direction of a beam of light is changed at the junction of two transparent materials, such as air and glass. When a ray at an oblique angle passes from air into glass, its direction bends away from the surface of the denser medium; it will change again when it emerges from the other surface of the glass, unless it strikes the junction at right angles. Lenses are refractors that focus light into a particular direction. Transmitting materials range from clear to diffusing; the degree of scatter, the shape of the surfaces and the transmittance of the material affect the final beam shape and intensity. The control of light by stage spotlights and street lighting lanterns is accomplished primarily by refraction.

Most luminaires use a combination of different forms of optical control to produce the light distribution required for a particular application.

The photometric performance of a luminaire is frequently given by two measures: the **light output ratio** (LOR), and the **luminous intensity distribution**, which is often called the **polar curve**. The light output ratio is the proportion of the lamp light output that emerges from the luminaire; it is expressed as a fraction or a percentage. For an installation to have a high energy efficiency the light output ratio of its luminaires should be high.

The intensity distribution describes the pattern of light emerging from the luminaire. It is frequently presented as a graph such as that in Figure 4.3, which illustrates the performance of a fluorescent fitting. The distance of the curve from the centre is proportional to the intensity in that direction. The two parts of the graph represent the intensity along the axial and transverse axes. The intensity distribution is usually described in terms of a lamp light output of 1000 lm (therefore intensity is given in units of candela/1000 lm). The reason for this is that the luminaire may be available for different lamp sizes; the user scales the intensity values according to the lamps used.

The photometric information provided by the luminaire manufacturer refers to a new and clean luminaire. Light output reduces through life with the changing output of the lamps and accumulation of dirt.

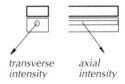

transverse intensity   axial intensity

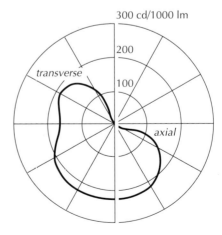

Figure 4.3 *Luminous intensity distribution from a fluorescent tube luminaire.*

Luminaires are produced by the lighting industry for a very wide range of applications. The designer needs to balance several factors when choosing luminaires for a particular purpose, and to anticipate the lifetime use of the installation. Table 4.3 lists some points to be considered.

Table 4.3 *Short checklist for choosing a luminaire*

Lighting performance
Light output ratio and intensity distribution

Electrical control requirements
Switching, dimming, automatic control linked to daylight or occupancy

Safety
Mechanical, electrical and thermal safety during installation and maintenance as well as during normal use

Installation requirements
Support, fixing, power supply, access

Maintenance
Frequency of cleaning and lamp replacement, eventual replacement of the complete installation

Appearance
Appearance of the luminaire in relation to the architectural design of the building

---

Sun and sky

5

For the designer, there are two distinct elements of daylight: **sunlight** (the direct beam), and **skylight** (the diffuse light scattered by the earth's atmosphere)

In hot dry climates and in the Mediterranean summer, sunlight reflected from the ground and other buildings is usually the main source of interior daylighting, but direct sunlight is excluded from rooms to reduce overheating and visual discomfort. In cloudy climates, light from the diffuse sky is used; windows may be large so that the interior has a broad view of the sky. In cool regions, although excessive heat gain can occur, the presence of direct sunlight in rooms is often welcomed by occupants for its warmth and brightness.

The sun's position in the sky can be predicted with great accuracy, but the strength of the solar beam – and whether any direct sunlight reaches the ground – depends on the weather. Even on cloudless days the presence of water vapour and pollution affects the relative intensities of sunlight and skylight. Where the sky is cloudy for much of the time, as in temperate and tropical humid climates, daylight is effectively the subject of random variation.

Forecasts of both sunlight and skylight illuminances in buildings in cloudy climates are therefore based on long-term measured statistics of daylight that give the frequency of occurrence of direct sunshine, and the frequency at which the illuminance from the diffuse sky exceeds any given level.

WHERE IS THE SUN?

The apparent path of the sun across the sky varies with time and place: it depends on the season of the year and on the latitude of the point on the earth's surface from which the sun is observed. The actual shape of the sunpath is the result of two separate rotations of

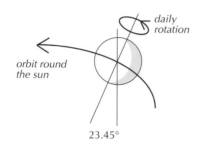

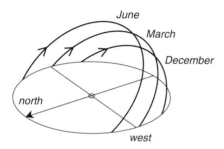

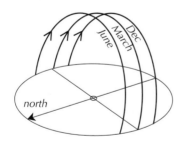

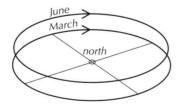

Figure 5.1 Rotations of the earth.

Figure 5.2 Apparent movement of the sun seen from London.

Figure 5.3 Apparent movement of the sun seen from the equator and the north pole.

the earth: the orbit around the sun, and the 24-hour rotation around the axis of the north and south poles.

Because the polar axis is tilted in relation to the plane of the solar orbit, the sunlight received at any point on the earth's surface varies during the year: this causes the seasons. The actual angle of tilt, 23.45°, defines the limits of the tropics (23.45° north and south of the equator) and of the arctic and antarctic circles (23.45° from the poles). This is shown in Figure 5.1.

On two occasions – the spring equinox (about 21 March) and the autumn equinox (about 23 September) – day and night are equally long, and the midday sun is directly overhead at the equator; it rises exactly east and sets exactly west. During the northern summer, when the sun at noon is overhead somewhere between the equator and the tropic of Cancer, the direction of sunrise is somewhere between east and north, and the direction of the setting sun is between west and north. The greater the latitude, the more northerly the direction of sunrise and sunset. During the southern summer the sun is overhead between the equator and the tropic of Capricorn; sunrise occurs between east and south, sunset between west and south.

The latitude at which the sun is overhead at midday is the **solar declination**, δ_s. It is +23.45° for northern midsummer, 0° at the equinoxes, and –23.45° for northern midwinter. The value of δ_s is used to describe the time of year in formulae to find the sun's apparent position.

At the north pole the path of the sun through the year is a gentle spiral. The sun becomes visible above the horizon in spring and remains continuously in the sky until autumn, reaching a maximum elevation of 23.45° on midsummer day. But seen from the equator the sunpath rises vertically; at the equinoxes it makes a semi-circle across the sky, passing through the zenith, the highest point. On the northern hemisphere's midsummer and midwinter days, the sun seen from the equator reaches a height of 23.45° below the zenith.

At intermediate points on the earth's surface the sunpaths slope across the sky dome, becoming more nearly horizontal as latitude increases. Figure 5.2 shows the daily paths of the sun as they appear in London, in comparison with Figure 5.3, which illustrates the paths at the equator and the north pole.

The maximum solar elevation (the angle of the sun above the horizon at midday) is

$$\gamma_{max} = 90 - \phi + \delta_s \text{ degrees} \tag{5.1}$$

where ϕ is the latitude of the site (positive north of the equator, negative south of the equator).

The time of day indicated by the sun – the time that can be read from a sundial – is known as **solar time**. This is not necessarily the same as clock time, for three reasons:

- Solar time depends on longitude – sunrise occurs an hour later every 15° west – but all clocks in the same time zone are synchronized. In Britain, for example, clocks are based on the average solar time at Greenwich, 0° longitude: so at Falmouth, 5° west, solar time appears to lag by 20 minutes.
- **Summer time** or **daylight saving** may be adopted. This is alteration of clock time to give longer daylight in the evening at the cost of a later sunrise in the morning.
- And because the earth's orbit around the sun is elliptical, solar time seems irregular by comparison with a perfect clock. In February, solar time is about 14 minutes ahead of a regular clock time; in November it is about 16 minutes late. This effect is called the **equation of time**.

Graphs showing the solar angles are called sunpath diagrams. The most common form is a stereographic projection in which the concentric circles give the angle of elevation above the horizon, with 90° in the centre, and the radial lines are compass bearings, or azimuth angles. Figure 5.4 illustrates the sunpaths for London in midsummer, midwinter and at the equinoxes. On 22 December the sun rises at about 8.15 am at 130° from north, rises to a maximum elevation of 15°, due south, then sets before 4 pm in the south-west. Sunpath diagrams are usually given in solar time, so they are valid for all sites along a line of latitude.

The outlines of window openings or of buildings surrounding a site can be plotted on a sunpath diagram to discover when the sun would be obscured by obstructions. This is done by finding the angles of elevation and azimuth from a point on the site to the corners of the obstructions. Various graphical aids are available to simplify the procedure. Figure 5.5 depicts the outline of a building plotted on the sunpaths for London. It shows that in mid-December sunlight would reach the point from sunrise until 11.15 am but be cut off for the remainder of the day.

The three-dimensional forms of buildings and their shadows can be cumbersome to plot graphically. An alternative is to use scale models with a light source to view or photograph the shadow patterns directly. A **heliodon** is a device that supports a model building, rotating it and tilting it as required, with an associated light source. The equipment is graduated so that the direction of the solar beam onto the building can be simulated for any time at any latitude. But no special equipment is necessary: a model of a building and its site can be illuminated with any suitable source, provided that the beam

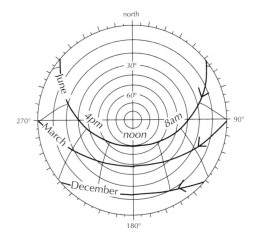

Figure 5.4 *Stereographic sunpath diagram for London, latitude 51° north.*

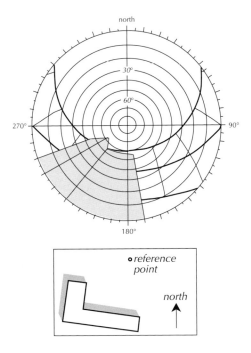

Figure 5.5 *Outline of building as seen from a point on the site, plotted on sunpath diagram.*

direction onto the model can be set up correctly. This can be done with a sundial – effectively a type of sunpath diagram used in reverse – adjacent to the model. Various publications on daylighting contain patterns for sundials; one especially convenient version fits into the form of a matchbox. The light source must be small, such as an incandescent lamp, and must be located sufficiently far from the model for the divergence of rays to be minimal. The real sun, with the model outdoors, can be used.

HOW OFTEN DOES THE SUN SHINE?

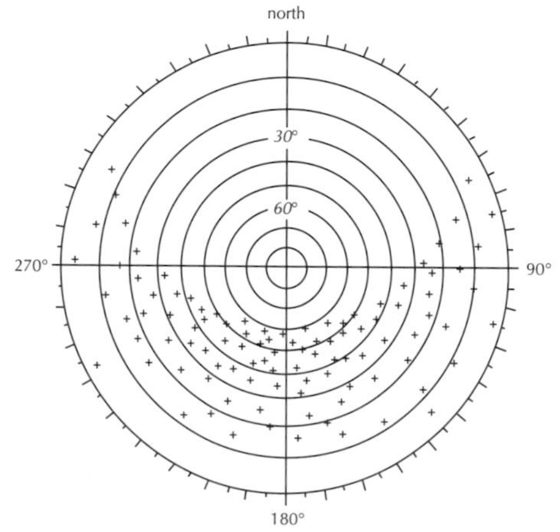

The sun is sometimes obscured by clouds, and this depends on the local climate. Sunshine occurs more frequently when the sun is high in the sky than at low solar elevations: a high sun tends to be associated with fine summer weather, but also a greater fraction of sunshine can pass through a broken cloud layer when the solar elevation is high.

Figure 5.6 shows the probability of the sun's shining from each part of the sky, taking into account both cloudiness and the geometrical distribution of the sunpaths. The density of dots is proportional to the probability of the sun's shining from a particular sky zone. There are 100 dots, so each represents 1% of **probable sunlight hours**. In London there is strong sunlight for about 1500 hours per year, so each dot also represents about 15 hours of sunshine.

If the silhouette of an obstruction is superimposed on this diagram, the number of dots visible shows the average amount of annual sunshine available at a particular point; this is denoted by the symbol T_{ps}. Example (b) in Chapter 16 shows in more detail how sunshine availability can be calculated, while Chapter 16 gives larger sunpath and probable sunlight hours diagrams.

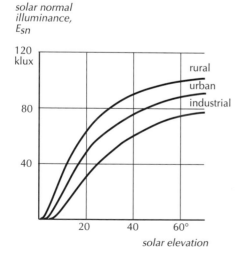

Figure 5.6 *Probability of sunshine in London. Each cross represents 1% of probable sunlight hours.*

Figure 5.7 *Illuminance on a surface facing direct sunlight, for different locations.*

ILLUMINANCE FROM SUNLIGHT AND SKYLIGHT

Sunlight is scattered as it passes through the atmosphere, even when the sky is cloudless. The lower the sun in the sky, the longer the atmospheric distance traversed by the beam and so the greater the attenuation. Figure 5.7 illustrates the relationship between solar elevation and **solar normal illuminance** (E_{sn}): this is the illuminance on a surface directly facing the sun. The graph shows that the clarity of the atmosphere affects illuminance, because the scattering is caused partly by water droplets and airborne particles. The term

turbidity is sometimes used to describe the actual degree of light attenuation, in comparison with that which would occur in a perfectly clean dry atmosphere.

The light from the diffuse sky excluding the sun is known as **skylight**. Figure 5.8 shows how this diffuse illuminance varies with the sun's height. Its quantity is far more variable than sunlight: in bright sunshine the solar illuminance is steady, but light from the diffuse sky can vary from minute to minute, and apparently similar skies on successive overcast days can differ greatly in brightness.

Long-term statistics can be used to estimate daylight availability in buildings. Figure 5.9, for example, illustrates the mean diffuse illuminance from an unobstructed sky in London. The variation by month and time demonstrates the strong relationship between solar elevation and the quantity of daylight, even when the sun itself is obscured. Knowledge of the *mean* illuminance throughout the year is insufficient to predict the periods when the available daylight falls below a certain level, and hence when electric lighting may be required. However, cumulative graphs can be used for this purpose, and Figure 5.10 is typical. It shows the percentage of a working day for which a given illuminance is exceeded through a typical year in London. It can be seen, for example, that skylight gives more than 30 000 lux on the ground for 20% of the time between 9 am and 5 pm.

The quantity of daylight entering a window depends more on the luminance of the patch of sky visible through the window than on the total illuminance on the ground. The pattern of sky brightness depends on cloudiness. In a clear blue sky the sun itself is the brightest point; around the solar disc there is a area of high luminance, which darkens to a deep blue in the area of sky opposite the sun in azimuth; then the sky increases in brightness again down towards the horizon. This pattern is used as the reference for skylight calculations in regions where clear skies predominate. It is standardized in a mathematical form as the **CIE Clear Sky**, published by the Commission Internationale de l'Eclairage, and is specified in two forms, for different atmospheric turbidities.

Under a sky with heavy continuous cloud cover the sun itself is invisible even though its position above the cloud affects the overall brightness. The lowest levels of daylight occur when there are several layers of cloud, and the brightness pattern found then is used as a reference for daylighting calculations in temperate climates. This is standardized as the **CIE Overcast Sky**. In this, the luminance of any part of the sky in relation to the zenith luminance is independent of the sun's position, and at a given elevation of view the sky is equally bright in every direction of azimuth. There is a steady increase of brightness, though, from the horizon upwards, and the zenith luminance is three times greater than the value just above the horizon.

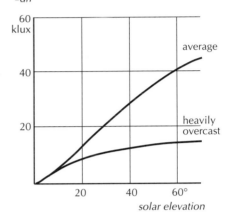

diffuse sky illuminance, E_{dh}

Figure 5.8 *Illuminance on the ground from skylight (diffuse light only).*

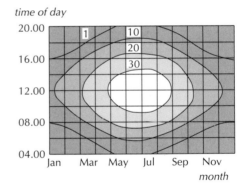

time of day

month

Figure 5.9 *Mean horizontal diffuse illuminance in London (kilolux).*

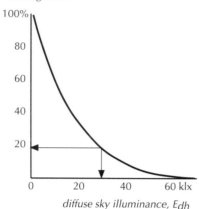

proportion of annual working hours

diffuse sky illuminance, E_dh

Figure 5.10 *Percentage of annual working hours (9.00–17.00) for which a given sky illuminance is exceeded in London.*

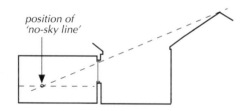

position of 'no-sky line'

Figure 5.11 *The no-sky line.*

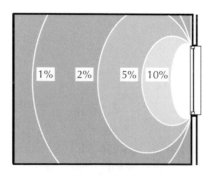

1% 2% 5% 10%

Figure 5.12 *Contours of equal daylight factor from a side window.*

The largest amounts of daylight are received from a blue sky containing big white clouds, because reflected sunlight often causes the clouds to be brighter than the clear sky they cover. Conditions change rapidly, as clouds are carried by the wind, or form and then evaporate. Although it is possible to simulate such skies in a computer model, calculations from these and other intermediate sky types are usually made statistically, using long-term measured values of sky illuminance.

The essential character of a daylit day is determined by the sky brightness pattern and the presence, or absence, of sunlight. We respond to spatial and temporal variations of light, so weather and time affect our perception of a place. The rate at which the sky changes can affect our mood: the visual pattern around us alters only slowly on a clear day and when it is heavily overcast, but rapidly moving cloud varies the light from minute to minute.

DAYLIGHT IN A ROOM

The amount of daylight falling at a point in a room depends primarily on the amount of sky visible from there: the greater the angle of sky subtended, the greater the illuminance. In an area of room surface screened from direct skylight (and therefore lit only by reflection) the illuminance is typically less than one-tenth that of equivalent positions near a window. The boundary of the area from which the sky is hidden is known as the **no-sky line**. It is illustrated in Figure 5.11.

Illuminance is also affected by the angle at which light falls on a surface. On desktops near a window the mean angle of incidence might be 30° from the vertical. Deeper into the room this angle increases significantly, until at the back the light falls on the desks only at a glancing angle.

These two factors – visible sky zone and angle of incidence – and also the fact that the desks close to a window receive light from sky nearer the zenith (which under overcast conditions is brighter) mean that the daylight illuminance on the working plane (a horizontal plane at desk level) reduces very rapidly with increasing distance from a side window. This is illustrated in Figure 5.12.

The light on vertical surfaces facing a window decreases less sharply with distance, so the back wall of a room often has higher illuminance than desktops close to it. On side walls there is a variation in illuminance, which depends significantly on the relative position of windows. The window wall itself, in rooms with windows only on one side, receives no direct light and is therefore the poorest-lit surface. The greatest contrast to the viewer occurs therefore between the window wall and the external view it frames, particularly of the sky. This can be the principal cause of glare from windows.

DAYLIGHT FACTORS

A window, unlike a lamp, does not give a steady flow of light: the interior illuminance depends on the brightness of the sky. The level of daylight in a room is therefore often specified by the percentage of interior to exterior illuminance, the **daylight factor**:

$$D = \frac{E_i}{E_{dh}} \times 100\% \qquad (5.2)$$

where E_i is the illuminance at a point in the room, and E_{dh} is the simultaneous illuminance from the whole sky (the illuminance on an unobstructed horizontal surface outside). The daylight factor is used to estimate the lighting in a room under cloudy weather; in particular it is usually taken that the sky resembles the standard CIE Overcast Sky. The contours in Figure 5.12 represent lines of constant daylight factor.

For calculation purposes a daylight factor is often split into three components: the sky component, the externally reflected component, and the internally reflected component. These percentages are respectively the light reaching the point in the room directly from the sky, from reflection by external obstructions, and from reflection by the other internal surfaces of the room.

Provided that a significant amount of sky is visible from a point, the sky component is dominant; it also can be simpler to calculate than the other components. It is therefore sometimes used as an assessment of the total daylight, particularly in town planning practice when considering the effect that a new building might have on the daylight available to existing buildings. Then D_{sv}, the sky component on the vertical external surface, is calculated; a method for doing this is described in Example (a), Chapter 16.

The **average daylight factor**, $\overline{D}$, is the mean daylight factor over a given area of the room, usually the horizontal working plane plus the wall surfaces below the mid-height of the window. It is valuable as a predictor of the likely daylit appearance of a space. Whether a room looks brightly lit or gloomy depends not only on the absolute quantity of light but also on the brightness ratio between interior surfaces and outside view. Judgements that users make about lighting are based on their whole field of vision, not just on a particular task area. The average daylight factor, which includes a measure of the total interreflected light, relates the general interior brightness to the visible sky, and correlates well with subjective descriptions of rooms – as described in Chapter 10, particularly Table 10.3.

The magnitude of the average daylight factor depends primarily on the ratio between the window area and the total area of walls, floor and ceiling. It depends also on the amount of sky visible from the window, the transmittance of the glazing, and the average reflectance of the internal surfaces. It is a very simple measure to calculate, and Example (c), Chapter 16, gives a typical case. The importance of the average daylight factor is that it can be used at the early design stages of a building to estimate the amount of fenestration needed to achieve good daylighting.

A daylight factor is a ratio and not an absolute level of illuminance. Furthermore, it is calculated on the assumption of a particular sky luminance distribution. To find from it an estimate of the mean diffuse illuminance at a point in a room under all types of sky, an empirical orientation factor (f_o) can be introduced. This takes into account the higher illuminances that are found on south-facing windows under all but very heavily clouded skies. Values are derived from long-term measurements; typical numbers for Britain are given in Chapter 16. Then, using the orientation factor, the equation for the illuminance at a point in the room becomes:

$$E = D f_o E_{dh} \qquad\qquad (5.3)$$

Used with graphs such as Figure 5.10, this equation can be used to predict the number of hours for which the interior daylighting exceeds a given level, and hence the hours of use of electric lighting.

Part Two

Designing

Information, control and energy

6

LIGHTING AND INFORMATION

Lighting design is more than the selection of luminaires or the calculation of window sizes: its scope is the composition of brightness and colour across the whole visual field. How a space is perceived or how a visual task is accomplished depends not on illumination alone but on its interaction with the enclosing form of the room and with the pattern, colour and texture of surfaces.

So the excellence of a lighting scheme is determined by many variables, and is assessed against many aims. Visual quality is not measured by a single value but against a range of criteria, which vary in precision and objectivity. Published codes give standards (particularly for task illuminance), and some can be legal requirements; but to satisfy these is only one of the aims of a good designer. Lighting can be complex and subtle, and inextricably part of the complete architecture.

Underlying all design criteria there is a single idea: **the purpose of lighting is to give information**. It is to enable the people in a building to perceive the nature of the space they are in, what other people are doing, and what they have to accomplish in a task. Our concern is not ultimately with physical illumination of room surfaces but with people's perception. And fundamental to lighting design is that *how* something is lit affects this perception. Only rarely is the user given the best information by flooding a subject with uniform light, and this is as true of highly technical requirements, such as close industrial inspection, as it is of drama in the theatre.

For an example, look at the Rembrandt painting in Figure 6.1. It is a biblical illustration, *The woman taken in adultery*. Although less than a quarter of the canvas area is painted in detail, the whole picture develops the narrative. The events clearly take place inside a grand building, rich and formal. The darkness of the upper parts, the actual absence of detail, is a clue to this; so is the gold sheen, the symbolism of the partly painted forms, and the relative size of

Figure 6.1 *The woman taken in adultery, Rembrandt (1606–1669). (The National Gallery, London)*

the people. Recognition of the central subject is immediate: the woman is brighter than any other area of the picture, and her dress alone is white; the Pharisees contrast in saturated colours and diverse detail. Christ is linked in hue with the people of the background, but is brought into the central event by the darker dress of flanking figures and by the gradation of lighting. Every aspect of light and colour in the picture carries information about the scene and the event.

It is no accident that we call pictures such as this 'theatrical', because they became a model for stage lighting. But the principle of selectivity is more general: the essence of design is to enhance particular qualities of the subject so that all that determines perception – light, colour, form – acts together to tell the story.

There are many measures of visual quality in lighting, but all can be expressed in terms of information. This is evident with simple criteria: the level of illuminance affects the rate at which fine detail can be assimilated by the viewer; glare inhibits the perception of fine differences or causes discomfort, which reduces attention; lamps with poor colour rendering mask surface colour variation. It is true also of criteria based on preference. For example, people tend to dislike windowless rooms because they are deprived of stimulation and knowledge about the exterior; satisfaction with daylighting may be related much more to the nature of its variation than to its absolute quantity. A good lighting design enables people to gain just the right amount of information: too little and the interior is boring and the tasks difficult; too much and we are confused or fatigued.

The following seven chapters show how light and colour can be used to reveal different types of information. Chapters 7 and 8 are about the room as a whole: how the brightness and colour of the major surfaces are related to the perceived character of the space, and how clues given by the lighting are associated with users' preconceptions about the nature of the room. Chapter 9 covers task performance. Chapter 10 describes window design: view, sunlight, light from the diffuse sky, and the relationship of these with occupants' expectations. Chapters 11 and 12 cover display lighting and exterior floodlighting: how light and colour can be used to heighten the perception of objects, and the practical problems associated with this. Chapter 13 describes the special case of emergency lighting.

In good architecture a building is successful at every scale, from its distant form within a townscape to the fine detail of materials and construction. Buildings are not designed for a single viewpoint. People enter and leave spaces, sometimes staying long, sometimes only glancing in. At one time the subject of view is a complete interior; at another it is a small closely examined part. There is vision from one space to another, and between interior and exterior. The relationship between light, colour and shape must be designed at every scale, from the distant view to the close detail.

The scope of lighting design lies across this full range, and it is important to emphasize this, because most published criteria, most codes of practice, are concerned only with detail and, in particular, with task performance. The quick checklist given in Table 6.1 sets the context.

Table 6.1 *Checking an interior lighting design*

Information

How does the lighting help the users perceive
> the character of the space?
> the architectural fabric?
> other people in the room?
> objects on display?
> visual tasks?

Control

Can the users control
> the view to the outside?
> daylight and sunlight?
> the general room lighting?
> the lighting in their personal spaces?
> glare?

Energy

How efficient is the use of resources
> of power and fuel?
> in installation and replacement?
> in maintenance?

LIGHTING AND CONTROL

When buildings are assessed after a period of use – the procedure of **post-occupancy evaluation** – it is rare to find user dissatisfaction related solely to deviation from standard design criteria. On the contrary, it is common to encounter situations where people are working without complaint in levels of illuminance well below code values, or with high glare, or with intrusive specular reflection. Conversely, a lighting installation can meet standard criteria but still cause complaints. This is because there is an additional, dominating requirement for user satisfaction: that the individual should feel able to control his or her surroundings.

Where this does not happen, the effects are measurable. Sick building syndrome, the occurrence of more than normal numbers of complaints of ill-health among occupants, is recorded most often where people believe that they have little control over their environment. Among office workers, perceived productivity has been found to be directly related to perceived control.

However, an inability to attain control – to open windows, switch on lights, or adjust temperatures – can be the result of inadequate design. The fault may be just the absence of local user capabilities, such as when all light switches are grouped in one place on an office floor, or where means of sunlight protection are not provided. But dissatisfaction is found also when automatic lighting controls operate without any opportunity for user intervention, particularly if the effects are sudden, as when lights are switched off, or if they appear unrelated to the local environment.

The extent of a person's control over his or her immediate environment is not determined by physical factors alone. Social interactions between users can reduce the scope of an individual's actions. For example, if in a workplace the means of changing the conditions of a junior member of staff lie within the immediate space of a senior then the junior member's actions may be inhibited.

In general, if a control operation affects a group of people in a room, the settings adopted can differ significantly from any individual's choice. There is 'ownership' of light switches, thermostats and windows, and this is subject to the rules of the society. People have expectations that are related to their membership of a group: in public areas, visitors do not normally expect to switch lighting on and off, and may be confused if this is required; in personal work areas some sense of personal control is essential to satisfaction.

LIGHTING AND ENERGY

Electric lighting uses a large proportion of the primary energy consumed by a large commercial building; in a building that is well designed thermally, the effect of lighting can be dominant. Part of the designer's responsibility is to minimize this load, and several tactics can be used: selective illumination (by lighting work areas more than surroundings, for example), efficient lamps and luminaires, optimum use of daylight, and control systems. Some of the techniques are described in Chapter 14.

But achieving energy efficiency in a building depends also on the motivation of its occupants. There must be an ethos of good housekeeping, of care for the environment; moreover, the people in a building must be comfortable in their physical environment, and must have the means of controlling it. People within buildings are able to make intelligent decisions about controlling comfort, and will act in response to aims such as energy saving provided that the methods of control are available and that the operating effects are self-evident. When the control system appears to be unresponsive to the wishes of users, the system is abused – either from ignorance or as a deliberate response to dissatisfaction. In practice, energy savings are related to perceived environmental quality. If this is low, applied constraints are counter-productive: misuse resulting from dissatisfaction can outweigh initial economies.

INTERRELATIONSHIPS

Consideration of energy, however, has a value beyond the concern for cost and sustainability. The achievement of fine lighting by the minimum means can be an intellectual aim, an aim akin to a desire for elegance in a mathematical proof or a search for a precise use of words in good writing. Information, control and energy are interrelated: the better the aims of lighting can be identified, the more precisely they can be met.

This is not easy. Building design is multidisciplinary, and projects extend over months and years. Many people contribute to the result; they may, for many reasons, not intercommunicate; and, between them, 'lighting design' has many meanings – from specification of electrical circuits to creation of the razzmatazz of Las Vegas. Therefore a designer does not work in isolation, no matter how specialized the brief. An essential part of his or her task is analysis of the interdependence of design decisions. Daylighting cannot be solved independently of the basic architectural shape; good electric lighting design cannot ignore the effects of windows; illumination for task performance cannot be done well if the character of light and dark in a room is ignored; colours and shapes cannot be designed without knowledge of the flow of light. Decisions made about each element of design are affected by others, because light, colour and form interact in their results.

Lighting and room character

7

The first step in lighting design is to establish the character of the room – the nature of the place as it will be perceived by its users. Interior lighting and colour give more than information about objects and surfaces. They set a mood, suggest an ambience; and this must be appropriate for the purpose of the place and consistent with the architecture as a whole.

But the relationship between lighting and room character is fundamentally subjective. Our perceptions of a place – judgements we make about it, feelings that we have there, even the extent to which we are consciously aware of our surroundings – are determined by our previous experience. Patterns of light and colour act as clues to the nature of a room by triggering associations with places experienced in the past. So we tend to perceive that a room has a particular character, and we also tend to express this in phrases that can be both physical descriptions and subjective attributions – expressions such as 'warm and cosy'; or 'dull', 'stimulating' or 'threatening'.

As designers we depend on the existence of these associations between particular physical surroundings and people's feelings, and on the fact that similar associations tend to be shared by many people. If they did not exist, or if there were no shared experiences, it would be impossible to design (or illustrate, or describe) a room that conveyed a specific personality.

The aim of this chapter is to list some of the consequences of these perceptual associations – factors within the control of the designer that can affect the apparent character of an interior. The first of the following sections summarizes the way in which memory and cultural background affect how we perceive the nature of a place. Then the chapter describes how

- the lightness and darkness pattern of the major room surfaces has a dominant effect on perceived room character;

- sources of light themselves – luminaires and windows – have a double effect: as objects in their own right and in their characteristic light distributions;
- surfaces within the room are important both in terms of brightness and in terms of their material;
- a room can be perceived as 'normal', its architecture then usually unnoticed by the user, or it can be perceived as unexpected and stimulating.

ASSOCIATIONS

A room filled with rich saturated colours and many small sources of light looks different from one of white and grey surfaces and uniform lighting. We see more than an aesthetic difference: the places seem to be quite different in character. We are probably willing to judge whether either is appropriate for a particular use because we have expectations about how rooms should look. These expectations are derived from experience, they change with time, and they are linked with the basic process of visual perception.

Groups of people with similar backgrounds have common associations between the pattern of light and dark in a room and its perceived identity. Substantial agreement is found, for example, if several people are asked independently to sketch or describe the appearance of a specific interior (such as a nursery classroom, a hospital ward, 'a haunted house'), and these descriptions concern lighting and colour as well as the form of the space and the objects in it. Similarly, when students in a lecture room are shown slides of interiors, they can agree on words or phrases that could describe each one – expressions such as 'bright and cheerful', 'scary', 'clinical', or 'sophisticated'. Perceptual connections between patterns of lighting and other attributes of a room are widely shared.

But they are not universal. Because they depend on experience, people's judgements are affected by culture and climate. For example, a large room with dark surfaces and small windows tends to be labelled 'gloomy' by students from northern Europe but 'cool and comfortable' by those from hot dry countries. And assessments are made rapidly, using just those clues that are available. They may change when more about a room is revealed; an illustration can be perceived differently from the real space, and an impression made glancing through a window into a room can differ from that of a person inside. Similarly, although the use of scale models is a valuable way of appraising a lighting project, the designer must take into account the subjective difference between the image in a small model and the character that would be perceived in the real building.

The process of perception is the linking of sensory stimuli with previous experience. The senses give us clues, but what we then perceive is the concept we hold that best fits those clues, not an analytical, television-like rendering of the physical scene. We therefore cannot assume that our own views or feelings are necessarily shared by others in a building; and lighting is only one of the physical factors that affect the perceived nature of a place (its effects are interrelated with all aspects of the architecture – the form and size, the materials, the detail). But the designer is able to affect the apparent character of a room, and there is sufficient generality within any particular culture to broadly predict what the subjective results will be of some lighting patterns. The first of these is the overall distribution of lightness and darkness on the major room surfaces – the floor, ceiling and walls.

IN A CAVE OR ON A CLOUD?

Rooms that are an everyday experience become a reference for all other interiors. Most familiar of all, for many of us, is the small or medium-sized room with side windows. Its characteristics are listed in Table 7.1. Such a room has been the most common interior form in temperate-climate buildings since the seventeenth century. It was illustrated accurately by painters such as Vermeer and de Hooch, and it remains the type of space most likely to be described as 'a normal room': it is the stereotypical living room, or school classroom or small office. It has a complex lighting pattern that we see but take entirely for granted. Figure 7.1 shows the illumination on adjacent surfaces from a small window; in addition to the effects of the flow of light from the sky itself, there is reflection from the ground outside and from many minor areas in and around the window opening. Further back in a room from a side window there is a gradual change in overall brightness as distance from the window increases, and a differing contrast between horizontal and vertical surfaces.

Now if we enter a room that has a pattern of light and dark significantly different from what we take to be normal, we tend to attribute to the place a specific character. Quite typically:

- surfaces with higher than normal reflectances, especially with light-coloured floors, are associated with interiors that are 'bright and airy' (such as the hallway of Ernst Giselbrect's primary school, Figure 7.2);
- predominantly dark surfaces are associated with 'enclosure', so if the upper parts of a room are very dark we might call the place 'cave-like'; if much of a room is too dark for us to be certain

Figure 7.1 *Daylit distribution from a cottage window.*

Figure 7.2 Primary school, Strass, Austria.

of its nature (as in Figure 7.3), the place seems 'mysterious' or 'frightening';

- richly decorated surfaces suggest 'grandeur', drab surfaces the opposite; if there is uniform electric lighting that masks the natural variation of daylight the place can be 'dull'.

Different building types have different stereotypes, and people's views (and especially the words they use to describe them) vary from place to place and from time to time. Part of the training of the designer is to sketch and record, building up a repertoire, observing not just the dominant patterns of lightness and darkness that occur in rooms, but also subjective responses to them.

However, an interior brightness distribution that is frequently found is not necessarily one that is preferred. For example, electric lighting in office buildings tends to be used continuously during daytime hours, but often with little room illumination from daylight

Figure 7.3 A man seated at a table in a lofty room, Rembrandt (1606–1669). (The National Gallery, London)

Figure 7.4 *Surface brightness in a room with recessed low-brightness luminaires.*

Figure 7.5 *Office lighting using luminaires with both upward and downward light output.*

itself. Many conventional design standards for offices are based on working-plane illuminance (the light falling on the horizontal desk surface), with secondary criteria intended to limit direct glare and minimize bright reflections in computer display screens. An outcome from these rules is the common use in offices of ceiling-mounted luminaires with strongly downward output, giving a concentration of light on the working plane, and vertical surfaces that

Table 7.1 A 'normal' daylit room

Floor
Typically the floor has medium to low reflectance, often the colour and pattern of natural materials. It is strongly illuminated in areas near the window, but may not be perceived as a bright surface.

Ceiling
The ceiling is usually the surface of highest reflectance, often white. It is lit by reflection from the ground outside and by interreflection in the room.

Vertical surfaces
The walls hold pictures, furniture, curtains; they are punctured by doors and windows; they tend to be decorated in stronger colours; the illuminance can be high in surfaces on which skylight or sunlight falls directly but low in areas hidden from the sky. Vertical surfaces vary in colour and pattern more than floors or ceilings, both within a room and between different rooms.

Directionality of light
Windows form large diffuse sources; their light flows downwards with a strong horizontal component.

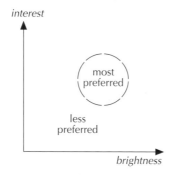

Figure 7.6 Schematic relationship between interest and brightness.

are relatively dark. This is shown in Figure 7.4, in comparison with Figure 7.5, which illustrates an office with luminaires designed specifically to place some light on the ceiling.

Despite adequate task illuminance, a room with only downward lighting is often assessed as 'under-lit'. In research examining the preferences of offices workers for various room luminance patterns, it was found that the rooms most liked had a 'bright' appearance, and this was related particularly to the wall and ceiling surfaces. Typically the chosen rooms had a mean wall luminance of at least 30 cd/m^2 (or about 200 lx illuminance on mid-reflectance colours). Assessments were linked also to the variability of the brightness; this was described in the experiment as the 'interest' of the light pattern. The interiors preferred above all others were those with both relatively high luminances and high interest in the broad zone seen above the desk working area, or the area most likely to be seen with a horizontal line of sight. Figure 7.6 shows schematically that, for a particular application, there is possibly a most preferred combination of brightness and interest. It is probably significant that the patterns found to be preferred are similar to those that occur in a daylit space.

Preferences for workplace lighting are therefore affected by more than task illuminance alone. For rooms such as offices it is useful to consider two separate zones, the **micro** and the **macro** fields, shown in Figure 7.7. The micro field is the task zone; the macro field is the wider 40° zone around the direction of vision.

Both are continuously in the view of a person engaged in a task. The needs of good task lighting may require the immediate background to be darker than the central task area (as we shall see in Chapter 9), but these must not override the needs of brightness and interest in the macro field.

Judgements related to surface brightness and room character are not dependent on the whole room being in view. We can make inferences from the parts that are visible, and often the clues we use are the patterns of reflected light. When major room surfaces are dark coloured there is little interreflection, and the total quantity of luminous energy within the space is small in relation to the light emitted from the sources. With high reflectances the overall distribution becomes diffuse: there is greater uniformity and greater total surface illuminance. A high-reflectance ceiling acts as a large source for the light it reflects, noticeable on objects below. The role of the floor of a room is particularly important because often it receives strong direct illumination, so a light-coloured floor may give clearly apparent upward illumination onto room contents and the ceiling, especially if direct sunlight enters the room. Often the nature of a space can be guessed when only the light falling on people or objects within it is seen – as in Figure 7.8, where the pattern of shading on St Francis' clothing is enough to describe for us the room as a whole.

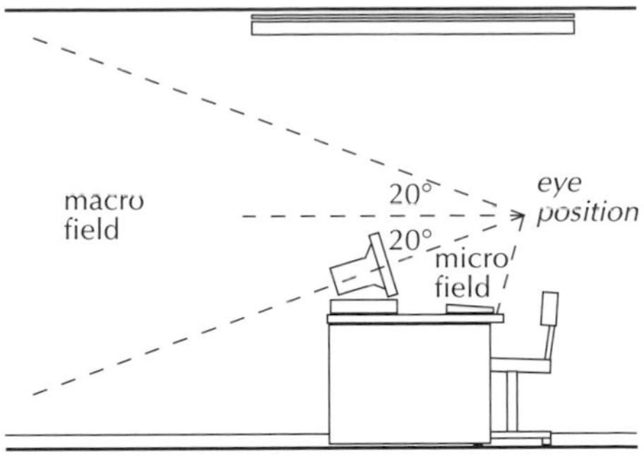

Figure 7.7 *Macro and micro fields of view.*

UNIFORM OR GLITTERING?

A large, low-luminance luminaire (such as a diffusing globe) can have the same light output as a small, bright source (such as a bare incandescent bulb), and equal total flux into a room can be given by a few powerful lamps or many small ones. Although each alternative might give an identical result if only a simple measure of lighting is used, such as mean working plane illuminance, the appearance of the place will be entirely different. The room shown in Figure 7.9 would change utterly if the many sparkling lamps were replaced by a few diffusing fluorescent fittings. And the qualities of the spaces in Figures 7.10 and 7.11 – electrically lit and daylit – depend essentially on the degree of variation in light and colour, and only to a small extent on the total quantity of light in the space.

Now consider the role that should be played by the light sources themselves. It can be an unseen part, where luminaires are hidden and the light that reaches the viewer comes entirely by reflection – such as where concealed lamps shine onto the ceiling to give indirect lighting to a room; or it can be an extravagant display – the rococo chandelier, the theatre facade. Historic architecture of all eras is full of examples to study: in the church by Jørn Utzon shown

Figure 7.8 *St Francis in meditation, Francisco de Zurbaran (1598–1664). (The National Gallery, London)*

Figure 7.9 *Small bright light sources and shiny surfaces.*

Figure 7.10 *Brightness and colour variation in a room.*

Figure 7.11 *Daylight modulated by vegetation.*

in Figure 7.12 (as also in many baroque churches) windows are hidden; compare the nature of the space with that in a mediaeval cathedral, such as Figure 8.1 in Chapter 8, where the stained-glass windows and other light sources (such as candles) are dominant.

Lamps and windows, as objects, carry meanings and associations. They are necessarily part of the architecture of a place. They contribute to the realization of a building's nature in a process that is both subconscious and part of an aware perception. They are a normal part of an interior, so if they are different, or apparently absent, we sense a difference. Certain specific forms of window or types of lamp can label a building; and some of these – such as the gothic window – are so long-established that their use can be a visual cliché.

Furthermore, we hold mental correlations between light sources as objects and the brightness patterns they throw; the size and shape of a light source affect modelling and cast shadow. A small lamp causes sharp-edged shadows and strong gradients of illuminance; a large source (in relation to its distance from the illuminated surfaces) causes soft shadows and gentle brightness gradients; multiple sources give overlapping shadows and complex brightness patterns.

SURFACES: BRIGHTNESS AND LIGHTNESS

Our perception of room character is affected also by the nature of all the materials surrounding the space. Lighting and surface qualities interact. For example, the luminance of matt materials depends only on the illuminance upon them, while shiny surfaces sparkle when illuminated by small bright lamps but look dull under large uniform luminaires, because they reflect images of the sources. To predict how bright a surface will look we need to know not just the incident illuminance and the overall reflectance but the size and brightness of the source and the nature of the illuminated material.

And, as we have seen in Chapter 3, we can usually distinguish between surface and illumination as factors in the final surface luminance. The luminance of a matt surface of high reflectance and low illuminance can be the same as that of one that is low in reflectance but strongly lit. But there is a subjective difference: wherever a source of illumination can be recognized, the nature of a surface can be distinguished from the effect of its lighting. A white ceiling does not seem to graduate into a grey-coloured one as the distance from a window increases. It is the phenomenon of surface constancy, the distinction between **brightness** and the **lightness** of a surface. They can be recognized independently, and in a room both contribute to the perceived nature of the space.

But estimates of both brightness and lightness are relative. Unless there are perceptual clues to the contrary, the lightest surface in the field of view becomes a reference for the remaining colours (because no real material is perfectly white). A uniform light grey ceiling looks white if no comparison can be made, with the result that the whole interior has a limited contrast range, perhaps a drab appearance. The inclusion of some high-reflectance areas within a room corrects this by establishing a large range of apparent contrast; this is one function of the white-painted architraves, window linings and cornices in eighteenth-century interiors. The portrait by Titian (Figure 7.13) illustrates the effect in a painting. The whiteness of the collar is not only crucial to the formal composition, it establishes the tonal range for the whole picture.

FAMILIAR OR UNEXPECTED?

Our perception of our environment is a continuous and usually unconscious process. Most of us, most of the time, are not looking with awareness at the buildings we are in: our whole perceptual mechanism allows us to take our surroundings for granted so that we can concentrate on a task. So the designer has the option of determining whether or not the normal users of a building become *consciously* stimulated by lighting and colour. It depends on the purpose: that is, whether display of the architecture itself is part of its function.

When an interior is to be a clear part of a commercial image, it may have to appear to be 'new' or 'fashionable' or 'original'. And if this is the case there are two requirements:

- to establish immediate recognition of the building type (if it cannot be identified then it cannot be appreciated as new);
- to ensure that it differs from expectations (if it is not different then it is not normally consciously perceived).

These are shops, restaurant, hotel foyers. Sometimes lighting must not only be creative, it must be seen to be creative; and to do this it must straddle the line between the familiar and the original.

But there are buildings where divergence from the norm is a serious fault. For people who are very old or demented, or partially sighted, unrecognized visual patterns – any variation from the expected – can cause an overwhelming handicap. For them, a lamp in an unusual position can cause utter disorientation; and there can be confusion between two and three dimensions: a change in floor colour may be perceived as a step; a wall and floor of similar colour with no clear skirting may be seen as a continuing plane.

And for all users there are some situations where clarity of information is essential: the building must be easily readable, because a

Figure 7.12 Church in Bagsvaerd, Denmark.

Figure 7.13 Portrait of a man, Titian (active c.1506, died 1576). (The National Gallery, London)

Figure 7.14 Trees in mist.

complex visual scene is overwhelming. In hospitals, and in buildings such as transport terminals, people can be fearful, anxious or confused. It is part of the function of the architecture to guide and to reassure. Lighting, colour and form must be mutually consistent, planned to sensitively and positively reinforce recognition. The best design is unperceived by the normal visitor because it is accepted and used unconsciously and automatically.

Where these constraints can be relaxed – where architecture may be displayed for its own sake – there can be complexity and indeterminacy. A great building is visually rich; at every scale there is more to see than the first glance reveals. As in an evening sky (or in the misty woodland of Figure 7.14) it is the half-seen, the subtly implied, the intricate, that is worth the continued gaze. In a building, the lamps and windows, the surfaces, the architectural form are constituents of a complete design, and all can be varied so that they interweave in many dimensions.

The dimensions
of colour

8

Surface colours (as we have seen in Chapter 2) can be described by three parameters: in the Munsell system these are **value**, **chroma** and **hue**. Each dimension of colour is perceived within a context of associations, linked with culture and fashion, but a colour system can be a framework for design decisions.

A HIERARCHY OF DIMENSIONS

Because there are three colour dimensions, there are three clear questions for the designer when choosing each colour:

- **How light should the surface be (on a scale running from black to white)?** The pattern of surface lightness and darkness dominates room character. It is important both in its direct sub-jective implications and in its physical effects on the distribution of light. If this underlying pattern is seriously wrong, no variation of chroma or hue can give a complete correction.

- **How saturated should the surface colour be (from neutral grey to an intensely rich hue)?** The degree of colour saturation in a room has, like the light–dark pattern, perceptual associations. A profusion of uncoordinated bright hues is a place for a carnival; a dark room dominated by a few deep intense colours is 'rich'; one dominated by neutrals can be 'cool and sophisticated' or it can be 'institutional'.

- **Which hue?** There are hues with inevitable associations (such as blood-red, leaf-green, or sky-blue). And in a particular scheme specific colours are often required – because they are already used in the building or have special meanings for the occupants. But choices of hue need to be related to the degree of contrast in the other dimensions. Variation in value and chroma can result in great perceptual differences, and when lightness and saturation necessarily vary greatly over the interior of a building, differences in hue may need to be limited. Restraint in the hue range can be used to give an overall structure to a colour scheme – to link spaces within a building and to control colour contrasts within individual rooms.

The sequence value : chroma : hue is often the hierarchy of importance. Effects along the lightness–darkness scale are described in Chapter 7, and these can be dominant in determining room character. By comparison, the result of only changing one hue for another is often a minor effect. But colour perception is complex: it depends on the eye's physical adaptation and on simultaneous contrast within the visual field as well as on subjective matters. Colour choice must be affected by these factors; key points are given in Table 8.1.

Table 8.1 *Some factors affecting colour choice*

Perception of a colour can depend on the brightness of the surface in relation to its surroundings.
For example, a small illuminated patch that looks yellow-red in a dark room looks brown when adjacent to much brighter surfaces (an orange and a piece of plain chocolate have approximately the same hue).

Perception of colour saturation is related to the size of a surface.
Few people, decorating their home, have not noted the difference between the apparent weight of a colour on a card of sample patches and its appearance on a wall. The larger the area, the more apparently saturated the colour.

Preferences are related to the length of time that a surface is in view.
Strong colours and large contrasts are preferred more in subsidiary spaces than in those occupied for long regular periods. In a school, for example, large areas of bright colour that are enjoyed in reception areas and corridors can pall or be distracting in classrooms.

The permanence of the coloured surface affects expectations of colour.
Vividly saturated colours can be accepted easily in ephemeral objects – the movable or short-lived items in a room such as fabrics, pictures and books. Surfaces that are to last the lifetime of the building tend to be preferred in the colour range of natural materials.

The history of the visual arts is a huge repository of experience of colour design. Knowledge of architecture is invaluable, but colour exploration in painting and graphic design has been, by the nature of the media, more extensive and more prolific than in buildings. As designers we can learn by analysing notable colour patterns wherever they occur. One lesson is that there are some strategies of colour choice that recur time after time; three of these are given in Table 8.2, and each can be a safe basis for a colour composition. But there are many others, and observation and recording are a key part in the development of a personal colour repertoire.

Table 8.2 *Some strategies for coordinating colours*

Adopt a hue range that lies within a small segment of the colour circle.
The Rembrandt painting in Figure 6.1 is an example of this. But the choice can be restricted to a single hue (such as on a single page from a colour atlas). This is a robust method of selecting colours for the main surfaces of a room.

Adopt two restricted hue ranges, approximately opposite in the colour circle.
In the portrait by Titian (Figure 7.13), the hues lie only in the yellow-red and purple-blue segments. A common technique is the use of small high-chroma areas centred on one hue with much lighter or less saturated large areas of the complementary hue.

Use large areas of white or neutral with small patches of bright colour.
Here the restraint is the limiting of chromaticity. It is a scheme that dominates graphics, especially the printed page, but is found in much twentieth-century painting and interior design. An example is given by the flowers and foliage within the school foyer (Figure 7.2).

COLOUR, LIGHTING AND SHAPE

The qualities seen in the choir vault of Lincoln Cathedral (Figure 8.1) depend on the complex gradation of light and shade. At this level, illumination is inseparable from geometry in architectural design. But surface colour and lighting can change the way shape is perceived at every scale:

- **Disparate elements can be integrated.** By being painted with a single colour, an interior wall irregularly divided by doorways and fittings can be visually unified; diffuse lighting can mask irregular textures or uneven finishes; a consistency of lighting and colour use throughout different buildings can cause viewers to identify them as a group. In the Burrell Collection (Figure 8.2), each space in this visible sequence has different lighting, but there is unity by the consistency of materials.
- **Chosen elements can be emphasized.** An architectural composition can be made emphatic by the differential colour of formal elements such as columns and cornices (a technique used notably

Figure 8.1 *Lincoln Cathedral.*

Figure 8.2 *The Burrell Collection, Glasgow.*

by Brunelleschi and Michelangelo). And minor components can be brought into display in a simple way by contrasts of brightness or colour, or more subtly by rendering them in a way that is unexpected. Oblique sunlight on the wall in Figure 8.3 makes evident every individual stone; and the fire hydrant in Figure 8.4 takes the attention not just because of its brightness and colour but because it makes a visual pun.

Such effects depend on the relative size of the components in the visual field. The integration of elements by common colour or lighting breaks down as the viewing distance becomes less and the individual objects relatively large. Conversely, as distance increases, textural and colour variation are lost; seen from a hundred metres the farm wall in Figure 8.3 is just a partly shaded surface.

LAMP COLOUR AND SURFACE COLOUR

The colour and direction of light interact with the colour and texture of surfaces. For example, the specular and diffuse components of reflectance frequently differ in their colour properties. The gloss on a surface tends to be non-selective in hue, so mirrored light may take the colour appearance of the source, while diffuse scattering occurs at a lower, pigmented, selectively absorbing layer. Under directional lighting this combination gives clarity to very subtle changes of surface shape, as in the sunlit leaves of Figure 8.5. Under diffuse lighting, colours tend to look less saturated because, from every direction of view, reflected surface colour is diluted with whiteness of the source. Outdoors it can seem dull beneath an overcast sky, even when the illuminance is very high, because colour contrasts are reduced.

Chapter 4 outlines how **colour appearance** and **colour rendering** are separate characteristics of lamp performance. Colour appearance is described by words such as **warm** ('fire-like') and **cool** ('as from the blue sky') . Numerically it is indicated by the colour temperature of the source. In practice, values below 3300 K are classified as warm and values above 5300 K as cold (showing the anomaly that the 'cooler' the source, the higher its colour temperature).

There is a tendency for warm sources to be associated with small-scale and informal interiors. Similarly, warm sources can be preferred at low levels of illuminance while cool colours tend to require high levels. But the colour, size and brightness of a light source and the nature of the enclosing building are all perceptually linked, and therefore, for any associations to be invoked, there must be consistency between the several visual clues.

Figure 8.3   Oblique sunlight on a farm wall.

Figure 8.4   Decorated fire hydrant, Berne.

Figure 8.5   Subtle revealing of shape in partly glossy surfaces.

The control of colour in lighting is essential in theatrical design, but its techniques need not be confined to the stage. Their use can be subtle: changes of lamp colour between one part of an interior and another can denote changes of scale or activity; they can denote a route, or a centre of importance. Colour variation can enhance perception of time, and mark the change from day to night; it can give clues about differences in temperature and be linked with other environmental senses. What is important is that deliberate variation must have meaning; change for its own sake carries no information. Accidental occurrences of colour difference within a scheme suggest poor specification or maintenance.

A lamp's colour-rendering quality depends on the continuity and shape of its spectral distribution. A lamp of warm appearance does not necessarily enhance a red surface, nor a cool lamp a blue surface, if the spectral power of the lamp is low in the range in which the pigments reflect. Colours in a room lit with lamps of good colour rendering tend to look brighter and more saturated than when the spectrum of the sources is poor. The room looks brighter, better lit; and there is some evidence that a greater visual clarity is evident, leading to acceptance of a lower illuminance than required from lamps of poor colour. There is also some related evidence that people will work under lower daylight illuminances than under electric lighting.

Task lighting

9

Reading a book, identifying someone's face in a dark street, operating a lathe are all examples of **visual tasks**. What they have in common is the need to detect and recognize very small parts of the total visual field. Often a task must be continued for a long period; sometimes the outcome of error is expensive or dangerous.

Most national standards and codes of practice for lighting are concerned primarily with task illumination. This, as we have seen, is only one part of lighting design, but it is a pervading part: there are few situations where the normal use of a building does not involve a need to perceive detail clearly. Ensuring that visual tasks can be accomplished swiftly and comfortably is a requirement in sports hall lighting, art gallery design and exterior walkway floodlighting as well as in the obvious cases of factories, offices and schools. Considerations of task lighting extend to buildings other than traditional workplaces, and part of the process of lighting design in every case is to identify visually demanding situations and specific task needs.

There are four important aspects of task lighting:

- task illuminance – its level and distribution;
- contrast within the task;
- contrast between the task and its surroundings;
- absence of discomfort glare.

Each is covered by a separate section in this chapter.

ILLUMINANCE ON THE TASK

Under a very low level of lighting, almost any visual task is difficult, and increasing its illuminance enhances performance. But

collecting on luminaire surfaces absorbs light. There may be a 25% drop between the illuminance produced by a brand-new installation and that from the system after 2 years of operation in a commercial environment. Recommended levels in codes are normally taken to be minimum levels in practice; the effects of ageing and dirt must be taken into account. In the *CIBSE Code* the recommended values are specified as **maintained illuminance**: that is, the lowest value that a system will produce in practice, taking into account the anticipated programme of cleaning and lamp replacement. The **initial illuminance** is that produced by a new installation (with discharge lamps this is taken to be after 100 hours operation). The subject of maintenance is covered in Chapter 14.

For rooms with overall lighting for visual tasks (such as general offices), there is often a requirement in standards for uniformity of illuminance across the actual task area – usually the extent of each desk or, if task positions are not defined, the horizontal working plane as a whole. Typically the required uniformity is that the lowest illuminance in the area should not be less than 0.8 of the average illuminance, excluding an area around the perimeter of the room (usually taken to be 0.5 m wide), which is often at a lower illuminance. With ceiling-mounted luminaires this is achieved by ensuring that the ratio of luminaire spacing to their height above the working plane does not exceed a given value, which depends on the type of luminaire. An example of this is given in the lumen method calculation in Chapter 16. However, where there is a variety of small task areas, or if a combination of general lighting and local task lighting is used, considerable illuminance diversity may occur across the working plane as a whole. It is typically recommended that the ratio of the highest to the lowest illuminance across the plane should not exceed 5 : 1.

There can be benefit in providing people with the means of adjusting the level of their task lighting. There is also some evidence that performance improves if a task is lit preferentially. This means that individuals can set the illuminance they feel necessary, and alter it for different activities. Not only do many workplaces involve several different tasks carried out at different times by different people, but the sense of being able to control his or her own working environment is important to an individual's job satisfaction. It is also essential to good energy management.

CONTRAST WITHIN THE TASK

The aim of good workplace design is to enhance crucial visual differences of brightness and colour, using both lighting and other means. An increase of contrast in the detail of a task means that a lower overall illuminance is required, and that the absolute level of performance can be better.

This applies particularly to silhouette-type tasks – the identification of shapes – such as reading printed text; but lighting can be used also to emphasize three-dimensional form, by creating shadows and by the differing illuminance that directional lighting gives on a moulded surface. It can highlight critical areas and mask unneeded information. It can be used to pick out minor variations in the shape of a glossy surface with visible reflections of the light source. Chapter 11 describes the enhancement of form in display lighting, and many of the techniques listed are applicable to task lighting.

Lighting in the wrong direction, from a poorly positioned light source, can seriously impair performance. This can occur when the wrong detail is emphasized, such as when a beam of light at glancing incidence enhances surface texture but obscures surface marking. The most common fault is, however, due to mirroring of the light source in the task. If a computer screen faces a window, the bright image of the window is superimposed on the screen image, reducing the contrast between one part and another. A brightness ratio of 100 : 1 between lettering and background becomes, for example, a ratio of only about 2 : 1 if a veiling luminance equal to the lettering brightness is superimposed overall.

The same can occur when paper lies on an office desk under an overhead luminaire, or a glass surface on a laboratory instrument picks up the image of the light source. Figure 9.2 shows that with ceiling-mounted luminaires above a horizontal working plane there is a zone (often referred to as the **offending zone**) where any light source causes troublesome reflections. To check this in practice, the task surface can be considered as a mirror: if any bright source would be visible in the mirror, it could reduce brightness contrasts within the task. Figure 9.3 illustrates the effect of glossy reflections in a workshop task.

Lighting alone is usually not the solution to improving visibility of very difficult tasks. Contrast on a plane surface must depend on surface differences, especially of reflectance and hue. Increasing the visible size of very small elements, sometimes with aids such as magnifying glasses, and giving greater black/white contrasts can be more effective than increasing illuminance.

Where tasks involve colour discrimination, either daylight or lamps with good colour-rendering qualities are required. If a task demands easy recognition of hue, the choice of lamps should be restricted to those with a good colour-rendering index (R_a of 80 or above; or, if accurate colour matching is required, an R_a of at least 90). But applied colour can be important. The use of colour coding in tasks, or a change of surface colours to enhance small detail, can

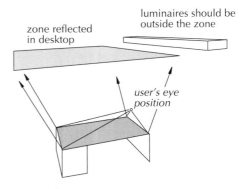

Figure 9.2 *Zone where images of luminaires are reflected in glossy desktop surfaces.*

Figure 9.3 *Gradations on a steel rule made invisible by specular reflection.*

be far more effective than improvement in lighting alone. Colour coding is especially effective in tasks such as sorting.

CONTRAST BETWEEN THE TASK AND ITS SURROUNDINGS

Task visibility is affected by the level of the eye's brightness adaptation. This adaptation, though, depends on the total visual field, and the task zone may be a very small part of this. Particularly important is the luminance of the broad area surrounding the direction of view. If this is significantly brighter than the task itself, the image of the task is 'underexposed' (using a photographic analogy) and its contrast range diminished. A very dark surround causes an 'overexposed' image, similarly losing task contrast. A quite separate consideration is the need to concentrate attention on a particular part of the field of view, which may demand much greater object-to-surround brightness ratios; this is discussed in Chapter 11, on display lighting.

The effect of varying the task-to-surround luminance balance is illustrated by Figure 3.2 in Chapter 3 and by Figure 9.4. When the background illuminance is about one-third of the mean task luminance, visual acuity (the ability to see small detail) is best. Making the surround either much brighter or much darker is detrimental.

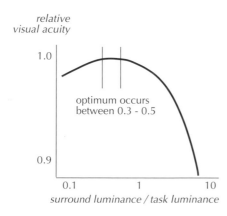

Figure 9.4 *Visual acuity and surround : task luminance ratio.*

The loss of performance due to very bright areas in the field of view is called **disability glare**. It occurs frequently in practice, without discomfort and often unnoticed by people at the workplace unless the task is prolonged and fatiguing. If a computer screen is positioned with a window behind, or there is a bright luminaire in the immediate field of view, the total amount of light falling on the eye can cause brightness adaptation to be at a level inappropriate to the task. Furthermore, contrast on the retina is reduced by optical scattering in the eye; the diffused light can cause a veiling luminance, a bright superimposed mist. An example in which the visibility of the central task area is reduced by bright surroundings is shown in Figure 9.5.

Shiny reflections in surfaces around a task are frequently a cause of disability glare. They are often more difficult to avoid than reflection of light sources in the task itself, because the surround area may be much larger. In a general office, ceiling-mounted luminaires need to have a low downward light output but a substantial sideways intensity, to minimize desktop reflection; but there must be a precise cut-off of this lateral output to minimize direct glare and reflection in computer screens. Such luminaires are described as having 'bat wing' or 'trouser leg' distributions because of the shape of their polar curves, as in Figure 9.6. When the positions of luminaires can be related to fixed workplace locations, glare control is easier. In offices a straightforward solution is to

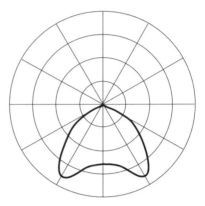

Figure 9.6 *Transverse polar curve of a bat wing distribution.*

Figure 9.5 *Task visibility reduced by bright immediate surrounding.*

Figure 9.7 *Features become invisible when a person is in silhouette against a bright window.*

ensure that rows of ceiling-mounted fittings run parallel to the users' direction of view, and are not directly above desks (as in Figure 9.2).

Scattering of light within the eye increases with age, creating a greater need for high contrast within tasks and low disability glare, as well as for higher illuminance. Everyday activities such as using stairs, recognizing faces or avoiding obstructions involve visual tasks that can be difficult for older people if there are higher brightnesses in the field of view. In particular, windows can cause disability glare in situations unnoticed by the fully sighted. An example is shown in Figure 9.7, where a person is silhouetted against a bright opening at the end of a corridor, making all features of the person completely unperceivable.

DISCOMFORT GLARE

Concentrating on a task when there is a very bright source elsewhere in the field of view can be uncomfortable. We try to avoid looking at the light, or half-close our eyes, or hold a head position that minimizes illumination on the face. Over a short period we might be unaware of this; but increasingly there is tenseness and muscular discomfort. In the long term, task performance is affected; but often we might not recognize the cause, and attri-bute it to other aspects of the lighting or to an unrelated environmental factor.

The effect is known as **discomfort glare**, and its magnitude depends primarily on four factors:

- luminance of the glare source (L);
- luminance of the background to the source (L_b);
- size of the glare source (measured as a solid angle, ω steradians, from the viewer);
- position of the source in relation to the direction of view (quanti-fied by a position index, p).

For relatively small sources, such as luminaires, discomfort glare can be quantified by the equation below, which gives the CIE Unified Glare Rating (UGR). This is similar to an earlier measure, the Glare Index, which it supersedes.

$$\mathrm{UGR} = 8 \log \left[\frac{0.25}{L_\mathrm{b}} \sum \frac{L^2 \omega}{p^2} \right] \tag{9.1}$$

The higher the value of UGR, the greater the discomfort: below about 10, any glare is imperceptible; above about 28, the situation is intolerable. A single step on the scale is considered to be the smallest difference that can be detected; a change of three steps is considered to be an interval of noticeable difference.

The equation shows the effect of varying the parameters:

- Glare increases when source luminance and size are increased
- Glare decreases when background brightness is increased or if the source is moved further from the line of sight.

Furthermore, the values L (source luminance) and p (position index) are squared in the equation, showing that a small change in either has a large effect on the glare rating. The graph in Figure 9.8 shows how UGR changes with the luminance of a single source.

Often there are several sources of glare in a room, such as an array of ceiling-mounted luminaires. The summation sign in the equation (Σ) shows that where this occurs, the luminance, size and position index of each separate source are combined, then the results are added up and inserted in the formula. In practice, glare can be calculated from data, usually in the form of tables, published by manufacturers for their specific luminaires when used in regular arrays.

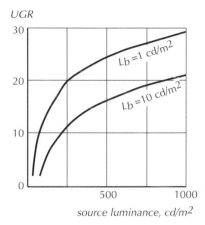

Figure 9.8 *Variation of discomfort glare with source and background luminances (single source, p = 5, ω = 0.02).*

IN CONCLUSION

Designing workplace lighting involves much more than ensuring that tasks receive a minimum level of illuminance; this is usually the easiest of the criteria to achieve. It needs the ability to visualize in three dimensions, because what is of primary importance is the geometry of the situation – the relationship between the viewer, the tasks and the sources of light. Failure in this causes the incorrect brightness patterns that give poor task performance and the direct glare that gives discomfort. In difficult design cases a mock-up of the workplace and the installation is a valuable means of testing alternative solutions. On site, the directionality of lighting can be quickly checked; Table 9.2 gives a practical way of doing this. Table 9.3 is an overall checklist of questions to be asked when approaching the design of a task area.

Every combination of task and user is different, and the first stage of the design process is to analyse the working needs. Often the solution incorporates more than lighting design. Especially with visually difficult tasks, the greatest gains in performance occur when small detail and low contrast are enhanced by changes to the objects themselves, by means such as colour coding, by changes to the whole workplace, such as providing a different background to the field of view, or by the provision of visual aids, such as magnifying lenses.

Table 9.2 *Four practical checks for glare at a workplace*

	Question	*If 'yes'...*
Shield the task from each light source in turn	Does task visibility increase?	The source causes loss of contrast in the task from veiling reflections
Shield the area around the task from each light source in turn	Does task visibility increase?	The source causes disability glare from bright reflections in the surroundings
Shield the eyes from each light source in turn	Does task visibility increase?	The source causes disability glare directly
Shield the eyes from each light source in turn	Is it more comfortable?	The source causes discomfort glare

Table 9.3 *Briefing checklist for task lighting*

Consider what characteristics of the task should be enhanced by the lighting:
Surface pattern
Colour
Surface finish or texture
Three-dimensional shape or silhouette
Motion

Consider the environment of the task:
Existing lighting
Positions of task and viewer, and whether moving or static
The visible background to the task
Constraints on position of luminaires
Surfaces in the field of view that could reflect light usefully ...or harmfully

Consider factors determining task illuminance:
Recommended standards for the task
Any legal requirements
Periods of task performance
Age and health of viewers
Consequences of error

What illumination is required in other areas? Consider:
General room lighting
Immediate background to the task

Can task visibility also be improved by other means? For example:
Colour coding or the use of magnification
Changes in layout
Removal of distractions

View and daylight

10

A window is a breach in the enclosing skin of a building, an opening for the flows – inward and outward – of heat, light and sound. It is often the element of a room that influences the interior environment most. Good daylighting is only one of the criteria of window design: for comfort there is also the need to control ventilation, noise transmission, heat gain and loss by radiation and conduction; and crucial to the architectural nature of the building may be the relationship between window, wall and structure.

For good daylighting itself there are several criteria. Needs for direct sunlight differ from those of diffuse light, and people's preferences for view and for overall room brightness are separate from demands related to task performance.

PEOPLE LIKE WINDOWS

Unless there is an obvious reason for excluding daylight, people are dissatisfied with windowless rooms. Almost any opening to the outside is better than none. A view into a drab courtyard or onto the back of another building is far from ideal; people may screen it with translucent curtains or indoor plants, but rarely will they choose to have a windowless space.

There are several reasons. These include fears associated with being underground or a need for an apparent escape route from fire; and there is a general feeling that associates windows with healthy light and ventilation. But, most importantly, windows give information about the world outside. Even if there is no direct view it is possible to infer the weather, the time of day and the activities of people outside from the varying pattern of light. Sounds carried through the window, and thermal changes, are also sensed; and, together with the varying light, they give an irreplaceable richness to the room environment. The changes that are sensed are significant not just as varying stimuli but because they have meaning.

But direct views can be essential, with needs and constraints that determine the location and detailed design of windows. Table 10.1 sets out a checklist.

Table 10.1 *Checklist for views*

Security

Is it necessary to observe areas around the building, or people approaching the entrance?

Supervision

Is it necessary to see out to supervise activities such as children at play?

Privacy

Is it permitted or desirable to allow view into the room from outside? Will windows overlook other properties?

Distraction

To what extent could activities outside disturb indoor task performance?

Glare

Are there bright sources in the normal field of view that could cause discomfort or disability?

Recreation

Can the view include some of the skyline, some middle distance and some foreground? Does it include obvious centres of interest?

Obstruction

Are there glazing bars or other obstructions at the user's normal eye level?

First come requirements for security and safety: the observation of possible intruders or the supervisory care of people outside the building. Then there is the need to control inward views. This is highly dependent on culture and room use, and even in residential buildings can range from a desire to display to a need for absolute privacy. Next, constraints on window design arise when a view to the outside could cause distraction or glare, particularly where visual tasks may be demanding and the occupants of the room are restricted in position; a lecture hall is an example of this, especially when visual aids are to be used.

Finally, when a view is offered for pleasure and relaxation, distinct preferences can exist. Research on this has been confined mainly to Europe and the USA, but within these contexts the following results have been found:

- People prefer views of natural scenes rather than of the built environment.
- A complete scene extends downwards from the sky to the ground near the window, and a preferred view contains part of every zone.
- Preferred views contain activity. In an urban scene, for example, this might be the movement of people on footpaths.
- When a direct view outside cannot be provided, internal windows giving vision into a space such as an adjoining atrium are normally preferred over complete enclosure.

An exterior scene may have a natural format that suggests a particular shape of window but, in general, preferences for window shape and size vary widely. Research results suggest that specific factors such as the position and activity of a person in a room and the relative position of items in the view determine whether, for instance, a window of given area should best be a horizontal or a vertical rectangle. Views change as a person moves around a room. However, the normal eye levels of room users are always significant – whether of child or adult, standing, seated or lying – because these should dictate sill heights and the location of horizontal glazing bars. This is an especially important factor in buildings such as care homes for the elderly, where the view through a window may be a person's primary link with the world outside.

In working interiors, such as offices, it is found that the preferred size of windows increases as the depth of a room is made greater. Table 10.2 suggests minimum glazed areas when windows are set only in one wall. An analogous result is that in a rectangular room a smaller fraction of the window wall needs to be glazed when this is one of the longer rather than the shorter sides.

Table 10.2 *Rectangular rooms with view windows in one wall: minimum glazed areas*

Depth of room from window wall (m)	Percentage of glazing in window wall, seen from interior
Less than 8	20
8–11	25
11–14	30
More than 14	35

DIFFUSE BRIGHTNESS

Windows designed to give a good view often let little light into the room. Sightlines look outwards horizontally and downwards, towards people and objects, trees and buildings. To have good illumination at a point in the room, the sky must be visible; and, roughly, the amount of light falling on a surface is proportional to the area of sky that can be seen from that point. This can be seen in Figure 10.1; here, the brightness of surfaces clearly indicates the window positions.

But the sense of a room's character depends not just on the illuminance at areas such as desktops but on the brightness of all the room surfaces. It depends on the total amount of light entering the room and on its subsequent interreflections. The interior shown in Figure 10.1 is successful because there is a high level of interreflection from light-coloured surfaces. Both the character of the room and the total quantity of illumination would be changed if the walls, ceiling and floor were of low reflectance.

The apparent brightness of a room from daylight depends above all on the brightness relationship with objects outside. Sun and sky change continually, and even if direct sunlight is excluded, the luminous energy entering a window can double or halve within a few minutes. But the subjective appearance of the room remains more constant: a room with small windows can look as gloomy on an overcast summer day as it does on an overcast day in winter, even though the absolute illuminance on all its surfaces may be ten times greater. The view of the outside – the brightness of the sky and of other daylit surfaces seen through the window – acts as a reference in our judgements of interior brightness. So the average daylight factor, the ratio of internal to external illuminance (as described in Chapter 5 and in Example (c) of Chapter 16), is a good indicator of room appearance. It correlates well with subjective descriptions of rooms.

Table 10.3 gives some guideline figures. An average daylight factor of 5% or more is found in rooms with a high proportion of glazing – perhaps a quarter of the total wall area in a medium-sized room. Such a room looks brightly daylit. The large windows may give noticeable thermal effects – overheating or coldness – and when the average daylight factor is much higher than 5% a room has the nature of a conservatory or greenhouse rather than that of an enclosed internal space. At the other extreme, in an interior with an average daylight factor lower than about 2%, any general electric lighting will tend to dominate over the natural light. The windows may be important to give occupants a view to the outside, but daylight variation on interior surfaces will be masked.

Figure 10.1 *Kettle's Yard, Cambridge. Illumination by diffuse daylight and interreflection.*

Figure 10.2 *Crafts museum, Delhi. Illumination by partly shaded and reflected sunlight.*

Table 10.3 *Room appearance and average daylight factor: values associated with rooms in temperate climates*

Average daylight factor	
5% or more	The room has a bright daylit appearance. Daytime electric lighting is usually unnecessary. High levels of daylight may be associated with thermal problems.
2–5%	The room has a daylit appearance but electric lighting is usually necessary in working interiors. Its purposes are: – to enhance illuminances on surfaces distant from the window, – to reduce contrast with the view outside. The use of daylight with supplementary electric lighting is often the best choice for energy efficiency.
Below 2%	Electric lighting is necessary, and appears dominant. Windows may provide an exterior view but give only local lighting.

These values apply to rooms with side windows, where a large proportion of the incident light falls first on vertical surfaces. With many types of rooflight most of the incoming light falls first on desktops or floor. This gives two differences from side window daylighting: the ratio of wall to working plane illuminance is lower, and a smaller glazed area is necessary for any given average daylight factor. Therefore the guideline average daylight factor figures for rooflights are higher than for side windows. For a wide room with horizontal rooflights in a low ceiling the values in Table 10.3 can be doubled; in other cases an intermediate value should be adopted, depending on the proportion of incoming light that falls on walls.

TASK LIGHTING

The principles of task light with daylighting are the same as for electric lighting: a minimum illuminance will be required, and the directionality of the light must enhance visibility. For task performance we are concerned with the absolute quantity of light falling on a surface, whereas for general room lighting what is important is the ratio of the illuminance inside to that outside.

A common method of computing the absolute daylight illuminance is to find the point daylight factor at the task, and then multiply this by the external illuminance and an orientation factor. This is described in Chapter 5.

For people positioned sufficiently near to them, side windows can give excellent work illumination: they act as large sources of medium brightness but with sufficient directionality to enhance modelling. The colour appearance of the light varies (but common experience permits the user to compensate for this), and its colour rendering is excellent.

The most important factor is the relationship between the direction of the light flow and the sightline of the viewer. Two things can go wrong: the view through a window can be too bright in relation to the task luminance; and reflection of the window in the task can cause disability glare. For both reasons the best arrangement is usually a window to the side of the worker, rather than in front or behind; this is especially desirable with display screen tasks.

A downward flow of light from rooflights tends to give less satisfactory modelling than side lighting, with a greater probability of veiling reflections in horizontal work surfaces. This is similar to the problem of direct downward electric lighting described earlier. However, the combination of rooflights with side windows in a deep room can be very satisfactory, especially where the rooflights are designed to illuminate vertical surfaces at the back of the room.

SUNLIGHT

Sunshine flowing through a window brings brightness and warmth. It can be welcomed with pleasure in a cold building or can be regarded as a cause of intolerable discomfort in hot weather. It is the most powerful source of light that a lighting designer can choose; it can be interreflected specularly, used directly as a beam, or used to create a bright diffuse reflection. For example:

- **Small, changing patches of high brightness, giving sparkle and contrast to an interior.** Of all natural images, few match the quality of woodland with sunlight penetrating the canopy, diverse beams making changing shadows on trees and ground, gleaming in patches of water. A shaft of sunlight in a room can be similarly modulated: by the glass of the window, the window framing; by blinds and curtains, semi-transparent or reflecting; by the geometry of room surfaces; by the surface materials – matt or shiny, white or coloured, flat or moulded. There is scope for complexity and surprise – the unexpected reflections on the ceiling, the interaction of surface hue with reflected colour, the drift with time of a sunlight patch.

- **Large sunlight patches in a room, probably important as much for thermal reasons as for lighting.** In cold and temperate climates, direct sunlight in a room is often welcome. In some conditions it is uncomfortable: visually, when it falls on tasks such as reading and writing; thermally, when the heat gain is excessive. But the use of direct sunlight is a traditional element of housing design, and passive solar heating is now a component of energy-saving architecture.
- **Sunlight reflected into an interior from surfaces outside.** In sunny regions, light from the diffuse sky is not the main component of interior daylight. Except around the sun, the luminance of a blue sky is often low, and therefore a weak source of light for the room; moreover, the sky itself is often screened from the window to reduce heat gain. The most useful source of interior illumination is sunlight reflected from exterior surfaces – primarily the ground but also from shading devices and other buildings. In this case the flow of light onto a window is predominantly upwards rather than downwards. Most of the light falls first on the ceiling; as a result the overall distribution of light within the space is more even than from skylight.

When people in cool climates have a reasonable expectation of sunlight in a room, both the size of the sunlit patch and the duration of the penetration are significant. Preferences for the area of sunlight tend to form an inverted U-shaped graph: there is an optimum size, typically 15–25% of the floor area, which is preferred to either larger or smaller patches. For a room to be considered a reasonably sunlit space, it was found in research in the UK that sunshine should enter it for at least 25% of the time that the sun is shining outside, with preferably at least one-fifth of this occurring within the winter months. The concept of probable sunlight hours is described in Chapter 5, with a calculation method given in Example (b) of Chapter 16.

Design for good daylighting in climates where the occurrence of sunshine is predictable differs from design for temperate or humid climates: orientation is even more important (because at low latitudes, heat gain is reduced by having windows facing north or south rather than east or west); external shading devices may be essential; and external surfaces should be planned to throw reflected sunlight onto the windows. Figure 10.2 shows how the different nature of daylight in a hot sunny climate induces an entirely different architectural approach.

In all climates, external reflections may be used creatively – sunlight falling onto coloured ground or water beneath a window gives rich hues or moving patterns inside. The quality of light in a Greek temple depends crucially on upward illumination from sunlit ground; this is shown, too, on the ceiling of the Palladian arcade in

Figure 10.3 *Cloister of S. Giorgio Maggiore, Venice.*

Figure 10.3. But the view outwards through a window to a sunlit facade can be glaring. A white surface in sunlight may be a hundred times brighter than an interior room surface; a glass facade, reflecting sunlight as a mirror, can cause the thermal and visual discomfort that occurs with a direct beam.

And in all cases, control of sunlight is essential. In dry climates the use of fixed shading devices or a good choice of building form and window orientation may be adequate. In cloudy regions – temperate or tropical – the occurrence of sunlight is rarely predictable so shading must be adjustable if maximum use of daylight is required. It can operate automatically (such as with louvres that move under photoelectric control in response to changing illuminance) or can be operated by occupants. A good solution can be a combination of automatic and manual control, which allows occupants to adjust blinds when they wish but prevents the blinds from remaining closed continuously with unnecessary use of electric light. Curtains or blinds can give the simplest sunlight control, but in warm climates this is inadequate; external shading gives lower internal heat gain.

REDIRECTING DAYLIGHTING DEVICES

Fittings such as light-shelves and louvres can do more than exclude unwanted sunlight; they can be used to redirect light, to increase illuminance at parts of an interior distant from a window. Direct sunlight can be reflected or refracted, channelled through light-pipes or down light-wells to spaces deep inside. Clear glass can be replaced by materials or systems that redirect or attenuate the light falling on them, either passively, as with holographic, prismatic or laser-grooved glazing, or actively with glass that responds to illuminance or to user requirements.

Such systems only control the light entering: they do not increase its total quantity. The amount of light entering a room can never be greater than the amount falling on the corresponding external surface, whether this is a conventional window or the receiver of a solar-tracking device. Furthermore, the incoming energy is reduced by the means of transmission, and the more complicated the system the greater the loss. Clear double glazing with normal dirt can cause 40% attenuation; the loss in a system of mirrors and light-pipes can be far greater.

So under a diffuse sky, the value of light-shelves, louvres or light-directing glazing is only a relative redistribution of light; there is always a loss of total flux. Usually the intention is to increase the light falling at the back of a side-lit room, but such devices can be useful for screening bright views, and can be part of unusual window geometries, such as occur in an atrium where strongly downward light needs to be reflected into surrounding rooms.

With the strong predictable sunlight beam available in dry climates the scope for flux redistribution is far greater. The need to prevent entry of direct sunlight is coupled with the need for diffuse illumination in the room. The total illuminance on each square metre of external sunlit surface can be a hundred times greater than the illuminance required inside. Even with substantial transmission losses, a relatively small external receiving area can give worthwhile interior lighting.

The use of redirecting devices does not alter the requirements of visual comfort, of a satisfying room luminance distribution and of correct task lighting. In some instances these become harder to achieve – when mirror surfaces are used to redirect light and when the changing position of the solar beam gives unusual angles of incidence. The measure of a daylighting system's success is not just the working plane illuminance; it remains dependent on all the criteria we have covered in these chapters.

GLARE AND COMPLEXITY

All means of daylighting can be glaring. When the source of light is outside a room the average luminance of the exterior is necessarily greater than the mean internal luminance. Because the view out may also be desirable and interesting we are likely to be more tolerant of this than of glare that results from a similar degree of contrast from electric lighting; but control of the brightness distribution from exterior to interior is the essence of good daylighting design.

Direct sunlight is the greatest source of possible discomfort. Falling on a task it can give a dazzling level of illuminance; in other parts of the visual field it can be intolerably glaring – if the solar disc is directly visible through a window, if it is reflected in glossy surfaces, or simply if sunshine falls on a light-coloured surface near the direction of vision.

But glare can also be caused by the contrast between the luminance of the diffuse sky and that of the interior. With an extreme brightness difference this can be a cause of discomfort, and in many circumstances disability glare can occur. We can use several tactics to ameliorate it:

- **Increase the luminance of the window wall.** Because glare is the result of excessive contrast, it is reduced if the luminance of the internal wall surrounding the window is increased. The wall

Figure 10.4 *Window in a medieval manor house.*

is better light-coloured than dark, and it requires a significant amount of light to fall on it, such as when windows in different walls illuminate each other, or when there is supplementary electric lighting, or simply when the total amount of daylight in a room has a high interreflected component. The average daylight factor can be a good indicator of this.

- **Reduce the luminance of the window.** This in itself is of little value if the total amount of light in the room is reduced proportionally. So when low-transmittance glass is used, or coverings such as blinds or translucent curtains, or external shading devices, there is usually a need for additional illumination.
- **Consider the location of windows in relation to the direction of view of people in the room.** Glare is reduced when a bright source is moved away from the sightline.
- **Introduce areas of intermediate brightness.** A sharp contrast – the sky seen through an aperture in a dark wall – gives the most glare. Glare is lessened when there are intermediate luminances such as light-coloured window reveals or curtains.

In the best daylit rooms there is more than just reduction of discomfort: beautiful lighting, as in Figure 10.4, is associated with subtlety and complexity in the total gradation from the sky to the darkest internal surface. This is not necessarily an even gradation. There can be small areas of high brightness, perhaps of sunlight; lines of lightness associated with variation in architectural shape; differences in translucency and colour. Above all there can be variation with time: a changing brightness pattern that responds uniquely to movement in the room and daylight and weather outside. All of this increases the information that people receive about their surroundings; it is simulating, reassuring and an enhancement of well-being. It enhances performance in the widest sense.

DAYLIGHT WITH ELECTRIC LIGHTING

It is rare in a large commercial building to be able to provide all the required daytime lighting with windows alone. The plan depth, in relation to ceiling height, makes adequate penetration impossible; and in those instances where full daylighting is technically feasible it is rarely the best solution economically, either on initial cost or on energy use. In the majority of present-day buildings, of all types, daylight and electric light are used together, and therefore should be designed to complement each other.

Electric lighting has two distinct uses in a daylit building:

- to enhance the overall brightness of a room, reducing gloominess and sky glare;
- to supplement the illuminance of visual tasks.

Because users judge the quality of lighting in a room at least as much from the brightness of the walls as from the task illumination, it is important that any control system that reduces the electric lighting as daylight increases takes account of the balance of brightness between the interior and the view through the windows. Room luminances should increase as the exterior daylight increases. Even if the daylight on tasks exceeds the minimum illuminance required, electric lighting may be required to reduce the brightness imbalance between the rear of a deep room and the areas near the window, and between the interior and the exterior.

When light from the diffuse sky forms a significant contribution to the lighting in a room (usually when the average daylight factor is 2% or more), its directionality and variation with time are appreciated by occupants, and should not be swamped by electric lighting.

No electric lamp can match continuously the colour variation of daylight. Apparent discrepancies in colour between electric light and skylight can be minimized by using lamps of intermediate colour temperature and by screening lamps from the view of occupants.

Display

11

Sometimes the main aim of a lighting installation is to enhance the appearance of things on display – emphasizing their special characteristics, making them points of attraction. Pictures in a gallery and merchandise in a shop are obvious examples. But the scope to brighten specific elements exists in every building. Living rooms, classrooms and offices need focuses of lighting, provided that these have meaning to the viewer.

The three preceding chapters have described different essentials of interior lighting design. These can be summarized as:

- determining the basic character of a place;
- ensuring that visual tasks can be done;
- ensuring that people have visual links with the world outside.

Display lighting forms a fourth component, and it is a requirement in every type of interior: the intention is to ensure that the eye is naturally attracted to specific elements – both objects within the space and elements of the building itself.

Lamps, luminaires and windows are part of the totality of a building, as objects themselves and in the lighting patterns they produce. They can, above all, be sources of decorative delight. They can be subtle, as where a concealed lamp throws an unexpected brightness; they can treat specific objects as centres of display; they can be flamboyant, as in a Regency chandelier or a laser show; they can be pure sculpture. The overall aim is to create a unity, with hierarchies of brightness and colour, in which chosen elements are dominant, where there may be complexity, where the essential natures of surfaces and forms are enhanced.

THE PRINCIPLE OF CONTRAST

An object is distinguishable from its background only if there is visual contrast: the greater the contrast, the more apparent the object. So if a particular piece in a shop window is to stand out, or a special picture is to be immediately obvious to a visitor entering a gallery, it must differ significantly from its surroundings in brightness, colour, pattern, movement, or a combination of these.

Where the aim of the design is to create maximum visibility for a task, we have seen in Chapter 9 that a ratio of task luminance to surround luminance of about 3 : 1 is needed for optimum visual performance. However, if the object is to have visual dominance over its surroundings, the contrast must be far greater. Table 11.1 summarizes the situation: where object and background are similar in colour, a 2 : 1 illuminance ratio gives 'just noticeable' apparent brightness difference; for a dramatic difference an illuminance ratio of 15 : 1 or more is needed.

Table 11.1 *Illuminance ratios for displaying objects*

Object illuminance : *background illuminance*	
2 : 1	Just noticeable difference
5 : 1	Distinct or significant difference
15 : 1 and greater	Dramatic or emphatic difference

The need for fine detail to be perceived in an object must therefore be balanced against the need to enhance the impact of the object when seen in its surroundings. The relative importance of these requirements depends on the situation: in a shop, for example, it is different from stage to stage of a potential customer's route. The purpose of the shop window is to catch the attention of potential shoppers and encourage them to enter the store. The window lighting is for attraction and stimulation rather than for seeing the product in close detail; this form of lighting borders on that of the theatre, and the lighting tools are similar. Inside the store, shoppers are attracted to particular displays with accent lighting, but then, making choices, they have a need to study items closely; and when purchases are made there is interaction between people, the need to operate equipment, and to write and to select coins and notes. In each situation the lighting must meet different criteria.

So design for display is related to design for task performance. The distinction is in the ratio of object to background brightness that is to be achieved. Changing this ratio alters both the extent to which the eye separates the object from its surrounds and the extent to which detail in the object can be perceived. Table 11.1 suggests the average illuminance ratio that should be chosen, but it can be no more than a guide because in practice an object on display can rarely have a constant brightness across its surface, and surroundings are rarely evenly illuminated.

The background can affect the perception of detail with both positive and negative contrast. If a dark sculpture is presented against a light wall the sculpture is seen in silhouette, and very little of the detail of the object is visible. If a white sculpture is seen against a light background, then because the luminance range is more limited, details of the sculpture can be appreciated.

Colour contrast can be used to increase visibility in a display, just as it can be used in task design. Hue and saturation differences (such as given by a red object on a grey background) can be powerful. They can be achieved by coloured lighting but more easily created by surface colour differences – and this gives the additional advantage that there can be differences in reflectance to enhance brightness contrast. However, a strongly coloured background can affect the eye's colour adaptation and distort the apparent colours of the displayed object. But this effect can be used to advantage: if a background hue is complementary to the hue of the object then the apparent colour intensity of the object is enhanced.

The eye is also able to distinguish a figure from its surroundings by pattern differences, giving another dimension of contrast. Pattern differences can arise both from variation of surface texture – which can be enhanced by directional lighting – and from variation of surface markings. The effect of pattern differences is greatest when the pattern change coincides with the boundary of an object. The converse – continuation of the same pattern over object and surround – can reduce the visibility of a figure (this is a central principle of military camouflage).

An object that is moving in relation to its background or that is changing with time (such as a flashing light) is especially noticeable in the peripheral field of vision. Movement can draw attention to an object that is not easily visible, especially if it is sudden or is repetitive with a frequency of a few occurrences per second. Such flashing, though, is uncomfortable to prolonged vision; slow complex movements hold the viewer's concentration once attention has been caught. Changes in movement patterns can be used to advance a person's attention from one area of display to another.

The four types of contrast described – brightness, colour, pattern and movement – reinforce the effects of each other. If all are present, the degree of each can be small and yet achieve a significant visual separation of object and surround. Table 11.2 gives a summary.

DISPLAY LIGHTING TECHNIQUES

It is easy to fix a spotlight so that it shines on a picture in a living room. Any reasonable amount of light will attract attention, and the

Figure 11.1 *The Taj Mahal, Agra. Enhancement of surface detail by strong sunlight.*

Table 11.2 *Basic contrasts in display*

Brightness contrast
The object is significantly brighter than its background, because of lighting, reflectances or both

Colour contrast
Object and surround differ in hue or colour saturation

Pattern contrast
Object and surround differ in texture or surface pattern

Relative movement
Object moves in relation to background, or its lighting changes

increased variety of brightness may enhance the whole interior. An element of display is present in most lighting designs, and can be simply achieved. But for sophisticated exhibitions, for museums, or for showing critical merchandise in shops, more analysis is needed. Consider:

- **What are the key characteristics of the object to be displayed?** What is it that has to be enhanced: three-dimensional form? texture? colour? Is the object delicate or sensitive to light?
- **What is the background?** Is it plain or visually complex, light or dark? Are there competing displays?
- **Who are the viewers and what are they doing?** Are they near or distant, moving or static? Is the display something they have come to see, or do they need to be attracted? Do they require to see the full detail of the object or just enjoy it generally?

Figure 11.2 *Henry Moore sculpture at the University of East Anglia. Enhancement of form and surface by low sunlight and clear blue sky.*

It is the nature of the objects that should determine the design of a display. A range of techniques is available, many of them drawn from photography and stage lighting, and each combination of source brightness and direction has a different visual effect. Ten techniques are summarized in Table 11.3, and several are illustrated within Figures 11.1–11.4.

Table 11.3   *Some display lighting techniques*

Silhouette
The outline shape of objects is seen dark against a brighter background

Halo
A beam from above and behind the display, shining towards the viewer, creates bright edges

Sparkle
Tiny points of light reflected by shiny surfaces reveal the shape of the surface and the degree of polish

Enhancement of solid form
A beam, perhaps at 45° in azimuth and elevation from the direction of view, gives large brightness variations across the surfaces of a three-dimensional object

Enhancement of texture
A beam at a glancing angle of incidence accentuates shallow carvings or surface roughness

Flattening of texture or form
A beam close to the viewing direction, or a large diffusing source, reduces perception of shape so that other characteristics such as surface pattern and colour can be appreciated

Lighting from unusual directions
For example: a beam from below reveals unexpected aspects of an object normally seen in daylight

Transmission
Lighting through translucent materials reveals the form of crystalline objects

Cast shadow
The shape of objects is revealed by shadows cast on other objects, or onto a background surface

Lamps within the display
Light sources form part of the display itself

Figure 11.3 *The importance of shadow and diffracted light in revealing crystalline form.*

Figure 11.4 *Royal Society of Arts, London. Lighting to enhance the architectural surface of brickwork. Designer Janet Turner.*

The various techniques can be used individually or in combination: the choice depends on what characteristics of the displayed object are to be shown. For example, tiny beams of light that enhance the sparkle of jewellery or the fresh appearance of food may fail to reveal the three-dimensional form of a matt surface; and lighting that emphasizes surface variation in low-relief sculpture can reduce the visibility of applied paintwork.

The matching of lighting to material is especially important in architectural lighting, for the enhancement of building surfaces. Rough materials need different directionality from smooth; and glossy materials take on a different appearance from matt materials when the size and brightness of sources are changed.

The absolute amount of light required on a display – the illuminance on the objects – depends on the luminance of the surrounding visual field, because the key variable is the ratio of object to background brightness. In dark surroundings a small heightening of object luminance is easily perceived; in a shopping mall there are many competitive displays, and for one to stand out not only is high brightness needed, but other display techniques, such as colour differences and movement, may be necessary.

But there are constraints on the amount of accent lighting that can be introduced. Remember that the human eye can cope with only a limited luminance range at any one adaptation state (Figure 3.2): very high brightnesses appear as dazzle, while all detail is lost in surfaces darker than the lower limit. Where good visibility is required over the whole display, luminances must be within the range associated with the adaptation level determined by the total visual field. Higher luminances are perfectly acceptable (provided that glare is not caused), but the designer has to balance the need for visibility of detail against the need for dramatic visual effect. Discomfort glare, as we have seen earlier, depends on the size as well as the luminance of the source, so very tiny high brightnesses can give sparkle without discomfort.

The positions of view and the activities of the viewers affect the illuminance required. The lighting needs to be more dramatic, with greater contrast between objects and surroundings, if

- the display is seen for only a short period, especially if viewers are on the move;
- the display is seen from a long distance or is only a small part of the field of view;
- the display must attract attention rather than rely on viewers' prior intention – if it is, for example, an advertising display rather than an exhibit in a gallery.

The range of viewing positions affects the choice and locations of luminaires. When there is a single direction of view, rather than an all-round view of the display, fewer luminaires are required, and direct glare is much easier to avoid. When people are able to move freely around a display, the beam direction of downward spotlights should normally not exceed an angle of 45° from the vertical, and the luminaire may require some form of baffle to minimize spill light.

The luminous intensity distributions of the luminaires used also affect brightness ratios, both within the display and between display and background. A very narrow-beam spotlight can light one small part of an object; a broad beam may shine on object and surround; a spotlight projector with optical control can frame the outline of an object, making it stand out dramatically. The shadow thrown by an object can effectively extend the display into the surround; and the cast shadow may be soft-edged, fading into the surroundings, or be hard-edged and precise; it can itself partly determine the ratio of object to surround brightness.

Specular reflections of light sources can seriously reduce the visibility of objects. This is especially a problem with pictures: a frame with glass is mirror-like, an oil-painted surface is shiny, and paper itself can be glossy. So, hanging vertically, pictures reflect images of lamps or windows behind the viewer. This makes it difficult to obtain even illuminance on the picture wall, because light sources should be confined to the zone shown in Figure 11.5, behind the reflection of the line of sight from the top of the picture. However, as the direction of illumination moves closer to the wall, the illuminance gradient on the wall becomes conspicuous – the wall becomes very bright near the lamps but dark lower down, with projections such as picture frames throwing deep shadows. Luminaires should therefore be positioned as far away from the wall as possible while remaining behind the reflection line, and it is an advantage if they have an asymmetrical intensity distribution that emphasizes the light thrown towards the lower part of the wall. Any rooflights must also lie in the reflection-free zone. In plan, light sources shining sideways onto a picture can be used to avoid specular reflections if viewing directions are constrained, but this is not normally possible when people are able to walk freely around a gallery.

The colour performance of the lighting equipment needs to be considered. Except when a theatrical effect is required, the light should have good colour-rendering properties – a colour rendering index (R_a) not less than 80. Often in museums and art galleries an R_a of not less than 90 is required, because accurate colour discrimination is an important feature of viewing works of art. It will also be necessary to consider the colour appearance of the light. Again, unless a dramatic effect is required a colour appearance (correlated colour temperature, CCT) close to the other lighting of the environment will be preferred.

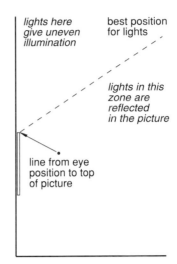

Figure 11.5 *Direction of illumination for pictures.*

MUSEUMS AND GALLERIES

The light received by objects on display may cause them to deteriorate. In addition to creating the visual conditions needed to study and enjoy the exhibits, the designer must consider conservation. This imposes a minor constraint with temporary exhibitions of low-sensitivity items, but is a matter of overriding importance with national collections in museums and galleries.

Lighting is not responsible for the most dramatic damage that occurs to museum exhibits, but there is a clear link between exposure to light and deterioration. This can be divided into two main areas: thermal and photochemical. Both occur primarily in organic materials.

Thermal damage is the result of local heating from absorption of radiation. This causes a loss of humidity, which in turn causes warping and splitting in moisture-absorbing materials such as wood and animal skins. The infrared content of a light source's spectrum makes the greatest contribution to thermal damage, and this can be controlled by the use of dichroic reflectors and other methods.

Of more concern is **photochemical damage**, the visible effects of which include colour change and physical deterioration. It is irreversible, and cannot be corrected by conservation processes. Damage to light-sensitive exhibits cannot be totally avoided, but it can be minimized by taking protective measures. These are based on controlling the energy received by the exhibits, and this is related to three main factors: the spectral composition of the light source, the illuminance on the object, and the length of exposure.

The most damaging part of the spectrum is ultraviolet (UV) radiation. Because this plays no part in the visual experience (except on fluorescent materials), it should be eliminated from the gallery – by UV filters on windows and, where necessary, with UV filters on electric lighting. It is normally considered that, except for tungsten halogen sources, incandescent lamps do not emit sufficient UV to demand filtering.

Deterioration caused by light increases with light exposure. This is a product of the illuminance (lux) and the length of time of the exposure (hours). For example, if the illuminance is doubled, the time in which a given amount of damage occurs will be halved. This is known as the **reciprocity law**.

Materials vary in their sensitivity to light; internationally agreed illuminance recommendations to limit deterioration are given in Table 11.4. In good conservation practice these are associated with a policy of reducing periods of exposure, such as excluding light when a museum is closed, and of presenting the most delicate objects only in temporary exhibitions. Higher illuminances than given in the table can be adopted if the total light exposure is not greater than the annual lux-hours specified. This is important to the use of daylight in museums.

Table 11.4 *Typical maximum illuminances and light exposures recommended for long-term conservation*

Type of exhibit	Illuminance (lux)	Cumulative exposure (lux-hours per annum)
Metal, stone, glass, ceramics, enamel	No limit, subject only to thermal damage	
Oil and tempera painting, fresco, undyed leather, horn, bone, ivory, wood, lacquer	200	600 000
Textiles, costumes, watercolours, tapestries, prints, drawings, manuscripts, miniatures, paintings in distemper media, wallpaper, gouache, dyed leather, most natural history exhibits including botanical specimens, fur and feathers	50	150 000

In museums many exhibits are displayed in glass cases. This provides the opportunity to control the environment within the case and to physically protect the exhibits. Wherever possible, the lighting equipment should be contained inside a separate compartment from the display. This allows the lighting equipment to be maintained without disturbing the exhibits, and to limit the effect on the display of heat from the lamps. Uniform illumination can be provided with concealed fluorescent lamps; low-voltage spotlamps can highlight features; a combination of the two is often the most pleasing. Fibre optic lighting is ideal for display cases. With this, a relatively powerful lamp is positioned remotely, and the light is transmitted to the display area via bundles of glass fibre. At the end of each fibre bundle there are optics that can focus the light and direct it to where it is required. The light is both cool and UV free, but the efficiency of the system is low, so it is often useful only for modest light levels. One lamp can serve a number of fibre outlets, but colour distortion can occur if very long fibres are used.

Reflected glare can be a problem with display cases. External lights are reflected in the outer surfaces; sources inside the case are reflected by the inside faces. This, again, places a constraint on possible luminaire positions. In low-light conditions it may be impossible to eliminate unwanted reflections completely, but every attempt should be made to minimize them.

Many museums stage **experience displays**, which aim to provide more than the viewing of a static exhibition. They may, for example, illustrate an historical period by transporting the visitor through a series of exhibits. Often called 'dark rides', these employ both sound and light; and although the objects on display are often genuine they are presented in a theatrical setting. Colour and projected light patterns are commonly used. The lighting may be animated to create the effect of time changes (such as sunrise to sunset) or of a fire or of sunlight reflected from moving water. The approach to lighting is very much that of the theatre, but there is an important constraint: lighting equipment must be concealed so that the illusion of the experience is not destroyed. Furthermore, several aspects of safety must be considered – both visually, as in sufficiently illuminating hazards, and technologically, such as avoiding the proximity of high-temperature luminaires and flammable materials.

Windows in a museum or gallery tend to be used for two separate purposes: to give people a link with the outside, and to provide illumination of good colour. The use of daylight must be considered at the earliest design stages, because it is dependent on the basic geometry of the building. If there are areas where very low illuminances are required, there must be transitional spaces for adaptation between outdoor levels and the gallery; if daylight is to give picture illumination, window locations are constrained by the need to avoid unwanted specular reflections.

Most old pictures were originally painted in daylight and intended for daylit spaces; many exhibits in museums were originally outdoor objects. It is in relation to daylight that the opposing requirements of display and conservation become most clearly apparent: for their long-term preservation, many precious items cannot be continuously shown in a lit environment that is historically accurate. But clever design can give a good simulation of the appropriate lighting. In particular:

- **Consider the adaptation level of the viewer.** The sense of brightness in a space is primarily related not to the absolute level of luminance but to the level of brightness adaptation. A room with moderately low illumination seems bright to a person who has a spent a few minutes in a darker space.

- **Consider object lighting separately from general room lighting.** The illuminance range in the room as a whole can be far greater than that falling on the object, and small areas of high brightness on floor or ceiling can have an insignificant effect on either object illuminance or viewer adaptation.

- **Ensure that the natural variation for daylighting is not lost.** Significant change can be permitted in the ambient lighting while the display lighting remains steady.

- **Use windows for low-brightness views.** Vision out into courtyards or gardens can be provided with little effect on interior lighting. Windows are especially appropriate in circulation areas and cafés; they also provide a means of orientation for the visitor.

Daylight varies continuously in spectral balance, changing greatly in colour appearance while retaining good colour rendering. It is this variability of colour that cannot be matched by electric sources, and should be the first argument for its use for illuminating works of art. Daylight is expensive to provide if its intensity must be regulated, and a complex gallery ceiling system of photoelectrically controlled louvres and blinds often fails to give natural-appearing daylight because the dominant characteristic – brightness fluctuation – can be lost. A modern automatic system can allow interior daylight to vary and still maintain recommended exposure levels, but the more rigorous the constraints, the less natural the lighting appearance. It is a dilemma that the finest paintings, which reveal most under the changing colour and intensity of daylight, are those that must be most carefully preserved.

The exterior of buildings

12

S o far we have considered daylighting and electric lighting of interiors. This chapter reviews night-time lighting of the exterior of buildings and of the areas surrounding them.

Electric lamps cannot match the sun and sky in power and size as light sources, so it is rarely the aim of night-time lighting to mimic the daylight appearance of a building or a street. The natural appearance is essentially different, as is evident in Figures 12.1 and 12.2: direct light tends to come from below rather than above; the sources are small points; there is negligible interreflected light; there can be sources of light on the building itself that are strong in comparison with the ambient light; and the sources can be brightly coloured. Exterior lighting gives scope for new creativity, the opportunity to design in light and colour on a scale that extends from the distant view of a town to the close detail of the building fabric.

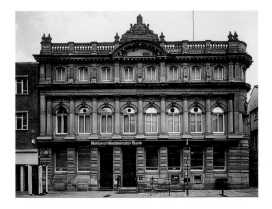

Figure 12.1   *Daylight appearance of a building.*

FUNCTIONAL REQUIREMENTS

Two sets of functional requirements constrain the design of exterior lighting: those concerned with enhancing visibility – because good lighting reduces accidents and crime – and those that ensure that exterior lighting does not cause annoyance or discomfort.

For a person walking, riding or motoring, recognition of the route ahead and the avoidance of hazards are visual tasks. The design principles described in Chapter 9 again apply: that is, a minimum illuminance is required, and contrast within the task must be appropriate. For the pedestrian it is necessary to ensure that hazardous places are obvious: steps, steep gradients, edges of soft ground or water. These need to be illuminated preferentially, with a direction of light that emphasizes changes of level or material. The use of surface marking, such as white lines, in conjunction with local lighting

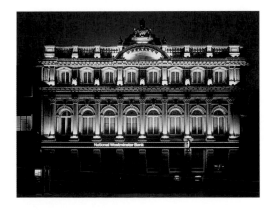

Figure 12.2   *Appearance under floodlighting.*

can be important in hazardous places. The motorist or rider requires in addition a longer view, and good roadway lighting is based on achieving two types of contrast: in the silhouette of other vehicles or pedestrians against a lit road surface; and from bright markers – lights or reflectors – on the potential hazard itself.

Clear visibility is also necessary for good security. A well-lit area receives less criminal activity than one that is dark and gloomy. Perhaps even more important is that people *feel* secure in an environment that is reasonably bright. To achieve this there must be continuity of illumination – no dark zones along a pedestrian route if personal attack is a possible or perceived hazard, nor unlit areas around the perimeter of a building where burglary might occur. Light must fall so that people's faces are recognizable, and so that doorways and other objectives can be identified. It may be necessary to illuminate for the use of CCTV cameras, in which case the lighting on vertical surfaces is especially important. If colour cameras are to be used, the lamps must provide adequate colour rendering.

But poorly designed exterior lighting can cause annoyance or discomfort. Inaccurately placed floodlighting can be glaring to motorists, and individual lights or illuminated signs can be mistaken for traffic signals. People who live in the vicinity of an installation are troubled when exterior lighting penetrates their own space: when it shines, for example, into bedrooms. This is often described as **light trespass**. To avoid it the designer needs to ensure either that luminaires are not visible from nearby windows or that the beams are accurately controlled.

Light emitted upwards into the sky vault creates light pollution – the haze of night-time brightness that is visible over towns. It is a serious nuisance for astronomers, creating a veiling luminance over the night sky. Some is unavoidable if there is to be any exterior lighting, because a fraction of all light falling on the ground is reflected upwards. But the installation of misaligned luminaires or those with inappropriate photometric characteristics not only causes nuisance but is wasteful of energy.

Table 12.1 is a checklist of functional requirements.

LUMINANCE, ILLUMINANCE AND COLOUR

The amount of light required for a night-time installation depends on two factors: the visual tasks involved, and the average luminance of the surroundings. Table 12.2 gives typical recommended illuminances for a range of situations. The principles of display lighting described in Chapter 11 apply to exterior lighting design: if a building

Table 12.1 *Functional checklist for exterior lighting*

Safety
Does the lighting enhance visibility of hazards, such as steps, kerbs, water edges and steep gradients?

Security
Are there areas that need lighting for prevention of crime or to give a sense of security to pedestrians or to people in the buildings?
Is lighting for CCTV cameras required?

Guidance and orientation
Does the lighting of pathways and drives indicate the route over a distance?
Are elements such as entrances, seats and telephone kiosks easily visible?

Glare, distraction and light pollution
Is the lighting glaring to pedestrians or drivers?
Does it confuse visibility of traffic signs?
Does it shine into habitable rooms?
Is light shining into the sky reduced to a minimum?

Luminances
Are the final luminances appropriate to the general area?
Does the design take into account any existing illumination of facades or streets, or internal lighting of windows?

Colour
Is the colour rendering of light sources related to the surface materials?
Does the lamp colour appearance give an appropriate sense of warmth or coolness?
Does the choice of lamps take into account any existing lighting?

Installation
Are the luminaire positions easily served by a power supply?
Can they be maintained easily?
Are they protected from vandalism and accidental damage?
Is planning permission necessary, or consent from adjacent owners?

Energy conservation
Are high-efficacy lamps used?
Do the luminaires have a high light output efficiency?
Do they illuminate only the areas required?
Are they switched to avoid unnecessary use, with automatic controls where appropriate?

---

is to be enhanced with floodlighting, or if an urban feature is to be emphasized, what is important is the brightness contrast between the subject and its surroundings. Figure 12.3 illustrates how ambient

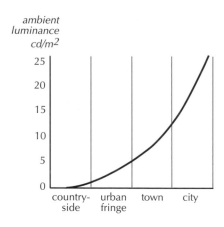

ambient
luminance
cd/m²

Figure 12.3 *Typical average ambient luminance due to night-time lighting.*

night-time luminance increases with closeness to a city centre. In open countryside no electric lighting may be visible; as a town is approached, highway lighting begins to give a general illumination; in a busy city street there are many sources – road and vehicle lighting, shop windows and signs, building floodlighting. The datum for design is the average brightness of the immediate area.

Table 12.2 *Typical recommended exterior night-time illuminances*

Purpose	Lux	On which surface?
Driveways to buildings, secondary pathways	5	Horizontal with at least 50% this value on vertical
Main paths, outdoor car parks	10	Horizontal with at least 50% this value on vertical
Security areas around buildings, main shopping streets	20	Vertical at 1.5 m above ground
Steps, footbridges and similar hazardous zones, entrance areas to buildings, recreational football pitches	50	Horizontal (vertical surfaces of steps should be differentiated)
Covered pedestrian areas, arcades	75	Vertical at 1.5 m above ground
Illuminated signs in low brightness districts	100	Vertical
Bus stops, coach loading areas, recreational tennis courts	150	Horizontal
Illuminated signs in high-brightness districts	500	Vertical

The illuminance ratios given for display lighting in Table 11.1 give a guide to the luminance differences that may be required between a surface and its surroundings. When an object or a surface is about twice as bright as the adjacent area the difference is just noticeable; a luminance ratio of 5 : 1 appears significantly different. When the ratio is more than 10 : 1 the difference in apparent brightness is emphatic – the lighting on a feature emphasized to this extent might be called 'dramatic'. Where several levels of brightness are planned within a design, equal steps in apparent brightness should be taken to follow an approximately logarithmic increase in luminances: that is, a sequence of relative values such as 1 : 3 : 9 : 27. Figure 12.4 shows the great range of luminance that typically occurs on a floodlit building.

Most external building surfaces are sufficiently matt to be treated as diffuse reflectors. Luminance then is related only to illuminance and reflectance (described in Chapter 1). In this way luminances from electric lighting can be compared with existing values of ambient luminance. Exterior lighting that is inappropriately bright for its surroundings may be considered a type of light trespass and a cause of neighbourhood dissatisfaction.

Many tasks do not depend on good colour rendering; it is predominantly the level of illuminance and the three-dimensional modelling that determine visibility, so lamps for exterior lighting may often have poorer colour rendering than normally required within buildings. But in city squares and shopping malls where people, the things they wear and carry, and the natural materials of the ground and the buildings, form many of the subjects of view, good colour rendering is an indicator of the quality of an installation. High-pressure sodium lamps are commonly used satisfactorily, particularly those with de luxe colour performance. Fine materials on a historic building may best be displayed naturally, using a white light with good colour rendering. But many inherent material colours can be emphasized – such as the use of red light on brickwork – and neutral surfaces such as concrete can accept a richness of colour that gives interest and complexity far different from their daytime expression. The creative use of colour is at the heart of good nighttime lighting.

Very accurate colour rendering is required for colour TV, particularly of sports fields; here metal halide lamps are the usual solution.

Figure 12.4 *Luminance variation across a floodlit building.*

BUILDINGS AND FACADES

Because night-time lighting on a building is usually from below, rather than above, and because the sources are usually close to the building, rather than distant, architectural composition for night-time is radically different from design for daylight. Inevitably, different elements become emphasized – for instance, it is the undersides of cornices and window openings, not the upward-facing surfaces, that receive direct light; there is much more variation in the incident illuminance over a facade; and the lighting is primarily by the direct beams, without a large diffuse source equivalent to the sky and with little interreflected light.

Table 12.3 gives an approach to architectural floodlighting design. The first part to be analysed is the context of the building – the principal viewpoints, the overall lighting of the area and of adjacent buildings in particular – and of the nature of the building itself, its scale and size, its urban symbolism.

Table 12.3 *Briefing checklist for floodlighting a building*

Context

From where is the building usually seen – both near and distant?

Is it viewed statically or from moving vehicles?

What is the nature and illumination of adjacent buildings and surrounding spaces?

What is the scale of the building in its context?

Architectural composition

Is the building seen at night from all sides or primarily as a facade?

What are the dominant architectural elements?

Are there any components, such as sculpture or lettering, that need emphasis?

Use and fabric

Is the building in use at night? Are the windows lit from within?

What are the materials? Do these imply constraints on colour rendering or colour appearance?

Does the building itself carry other external lighting, such as signs or roadway lanterns?

Location of luminaires

In what positions can luminaires be placed, considering power supply, access and protection?

What are the requirements of daytime appearance? Can the luminaires be screened from view?

Then comes an appraisal of the building's form. In all lighting design the key is selectivity – not flooding every surface with even illumination but building up a pattern of gradations from light to dark, giving emphasis to some elements, masking others. For external lighting the form of the surrounding spaces is relevant, especially in determining the regions of the building to be treated. Frequently in central urban streets and squares it is only the facades of the enclosing buildings that are illuminated.

Existing lighting on the building is a constraint; this can be from within, giving windows that are lit at night, or external fittings that provide street lighting. A further constraint on design, and often a dominating one, is the restriction of luminaire locations, particularly where these have to be attached to the building itself or be very close to it.

It is a general principle that the more distant a lamp is from the surface it illuminates, the more uniform the illuminance across the surface. In addition, the angle of incidence determines the extent to which texture is enhanced – when light falls perpendicular onto a surface, irregularities are masked. So the closer to a building facade any floodlighting lanterns are placed, the greater the diversity will be across the surface; the more dramatic will the appearance be, because the contrast range is greater; and the more the textural qualities of the material will be emphasized.

In the same way, the use of shadows is essential in the modelling of a facade. If a building is lit from the viewing position it will appear flat and unappealing. The luminaires need to be positioned away from the viewing direction so that three-dimensional elements on the building facade will be shown in relief. For vertical elements such as pilasters to be visible, the floodlights need to be positioned so that small shadows are thrown to one side of them. The angle will be determined by the depth of the elements but an angle of 45° is a good starting point. If the angle is too shallow then the shadows will be excessive. These lanterns may be supplemented by others that are aimed from the opposite direction to soften a particularly deep shadow. However, these need to provide a lower illuminance to avoid obliterating the shadows completely. If the building has horizontal elements such as an architrave or cornice then the flood-lights should be aimed upwards to project a small shadow above the element. The width of the shadow will be determined by the distance of the lanterns from the building.

If a complete building or a major element such as a dome is to be illuminated and seen from several directions, its three-dimensional form becomes fully apparent only when there is variation in the lighting from the different directions. This is shown by several build-ings in the view of the floodlit Acropolis in Athens (cover picture). It can also be seen that for the enhancement of form the luminance difference between adjacent faces can be subtle. This is particularly clear in the lighting of the retaining walls beneath the Parthenon; the positions chosen for the luminaires also cause the wall texture to be enhanced.

Areas of darkness and shadow are part of a good design; they serve the same function as silences in music, framing a piece and punctuating it. Their importance is evident in the overall view of Athens; the clear dominance of the Acropolis depends on the rela-tive darkness of the surrounding city. Darkness enables silhouettes to be created, often a valuable technique for outlining a complete building or a tree, as in Figure 12.5. Silhouette is also useful for displaying individual elements, such as the columns in front of an illuminated portico.

When only individual elements of a large building are highlighted it may be necessary to ensure that the total shape is perceptible, either by a low level of illumination over large parts of it or by tracing the form with lines of light. Isolated patches of brightness, especially those high up on a building, can be visually incongruous:

Figure 12.5 *Newark Castle.*

they apparently float in the air or seem part of another structure. Conversely, by not lighting the roof and other upper parts of a building, the form can seem to disappear into the night sky.

Just as the pattern of light and dark on a floodlit building is usually different from its daytime appearance, with a far greater contrast range, so night-time colour can be different. A much enhanced palette is available to the designer. Lamps and trans-illuminated materials in signs and displays can have a brilliant intensity of colour; patterns of light and colour can be made to move; the whole composition can alter with time or respond to its environment. The interior of a building can be part of the exterior scene by night, in a way impossible by day (as in Figure 12.6).

To help with the development of a design, shaded perspective sketches can be valuable. These may be used not only as a design aid but as a way of conveying the final proposal to the client.

Figure 12.6 *De Vere Grand Harbour Hotel, Southampton. Lighting designer Maurice Brill.*

PEDESTRIAN ROUTES AND SURROUNDING AREAS

One of the functions of night-time lighting is to provide a means of direction-finding. At the large scale, important buildings that are floodlit can serve this purpose, making it possible for strangers within a city to orientate themselves. At an intermediate scale the routes themselves may have to be easily identifiable for a distance ahead – as when a path threads through a park, or a safe pedestrian way needs to be indicated in an area where there is vehicular traffic. Luminaires can act as beacons even if they cast little light onto the ground.

The key to good design for pedestrian areas is to imagine (or draw in perspective) the view from a succession of points along a route, checking not only the requirements for safety and security but how the distant prospect varies and how particular features move in and out of view. Variety is essential to an interesting route, and this depends on the lighting as well as on the objects illuminated. For example, in a pedestrian shopping centre the general lighting might be provided by high-mounted luminaires to give a wash of light over the area. This could be supplemented by lighting the pedestrian walkways with low bollards. Visual accents could be engineered by illuminating elements of the landscape such as trees and flower beds, or architectural features such as statues. Fountains and other water features are always popular, although they will require a high level of maintenance. This form of lighting is best done by lighting up into the water jets from below the surface. This will mean using equipment that is suitable for underwater use. Fibre optic lighting is a good solution as it keeps the lamp and the luminaire electrical components away from the water and therefore avoids a potentially hazardous situation; the maintenance is also much easier. Persuading shopkeepers to provide some illumination in the shop windows at night creates another important and attractive feature. Illuminated signs, and illuminated decorations at Christmas, are other possibilities. The extent is endless, and is limited only by the designer's inventiveness.

THE OVERALL VIEW

The night-time lighting of a town needs to be considered holistically. Floodlit buildings can be visible for many miles, and each is seen not just against its immediate neighbours but in the context of a whole urban composition. This composition must be coherent: the brightest and most colourful parts must be chosen, not accidental; secondary buildings must not be made inappropriately dominant; there must be areas of shade as well as centres of brightness; major three-dimensional elements – great buildings, or the natural topography – must not be visually flattened with lighting that is uniform around all sides.

Achieving this may require the overall control of a local authority. Every town contains a range of different buildings and activities, so conflicts of aims can arise: an over-lit commercial building can overwhelm an adjacent historic monument; and the illuminated advertising sign of a leisure complex in a suburban district can appear brash and intrusive. The current thinking is that some form of planning control on exterior lighting is necessary, at least to protect the environment from the worst excesses of bad lighting, including light pollution in all its forms.

DAYTIME APPEARANCE, ENERGY EFFICIENCY AND MAINTENANCE

Lighting fittings can be a noticeable part of the urban picture in daylight. Their appearance and the way they are integrated with the surrounding architecture and with other items in the street must be considered in the early stages of design. Luminaires for floodlighting can often be screened from normal directions of view – hidden within planting, sunk into the ground in purpose-built pits with a glass covering, or concealed in other street furniture. When fittings are mounted on buildings, their style must be appropriate to the architecture, and their placing must be part of the overall architectural design. Figure 12.7 is an example of the way in which luminaires can be incorporated within a large structure; in this case it is the semi-outdoor roof of a railway station.

For energy efficiency the lamps selected must have a high efficacy; this normally implies the use of discharge lamps. The luminaires must emit a high proportion of the lamp light output and have an intensity distribution to light only the areas required. Automatic lighting controls usually form an element of the design. Photocell-operated switches can be used to switch lamps on at dusk and off at dawn, and can be used with time controls to switch lamps off at some point during the night. Occupancy sensors can be used for access lighting to switch lamps on as someone approaches a building, although when instant light is required high-pressure discharge lamps are unsuitable because of their long run-up time.

Maintenance is another important subject. Exterior lighting equipment is required to operate under severe weather conditions for many years, and hence must be weatherproof to withstand the ingress of water and dirt. This aspect of a luminaire performance is described by its ingress protection (IP) rating. Nonetheless, luminaires need to be cleaned and maintained for a satisfactory performance at all times. Failed lamps have to be replaced. To ensure that maintenance is carried out quickly and efficiently the equipment needs to be easily accessible, and a maintenance plan must be developed with the client: without a proper plan an installation will quickly deteriorate.

Sadly, vandalism can be a problem, particularly if the equipment is easily accessible. Equipment needs to be selected with this in mind, using, for instance, robust materials with a high impact resistance and fixings that are tamper-proof.

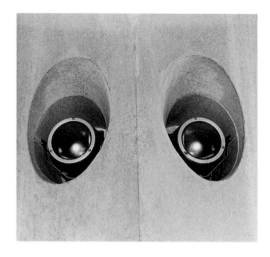

Figure 12.7 *Railway station, Lyon, France. Integration of floodlighting luminaire with structure. Designer Santiago Calatrava.*

Emergency lighting

13

The purpose of emergency lighting is to provide safety for the occupants of a building in the case of a failure to the normal lighting electrical supply. The supply failure may be caused by a simple electrical fault or, more extremely, by fire engulfing the building. Because of this, emergency lighting must be powered from an independent supply, which switches on automatically when required. Its main purposes are to enable people to

- evacuate a building safely;
- shut down hazardous processes;
- continue vital activities.

In every case the illumination must be sufficient for the purpose, and must operate long enough for the procedures to be accomplished with safety.

Emergency lighting is required in buildings where the public have access, in commercial and industrial workplaces, and in buildings such as hospitals and residential homes. There are minimum standards for emergency lighting, which are governed by legislation, and the designer must consult the current standards for the area and type of building being designed. It is important to note that different standards apply in different countries.

ESCAPE LIGHTING

If the normal building lighting fails and people are plunged into darkness there is a real possibility of panic and accidents, which could be fatal. Under these conditions it is essential that the emergency escape lighting switches on immediately, or at least in a very few seconds. The escape lighting must provide sufficient light for people to identify the escape route and to be able to move quickly along it to the outside, avoiding any hazards on the way. Because the emergency light level is usually at a much lower illuminance than that from the normal lighting, people take time to adapt. The escape route needs to be relatively evenly lit. In particular, the lighting should

- indicate changes of direction or level, including stairs;
- ensure that fire-fighting and other safety equipment can be quickly and clearly recognized;
- provide sufficient illumination in open areas, such as open-plan offices, for occupants to move quickly towards their designated escape route.

Illuminated direction signs (which have their own standard specifications) are part of an escape route lighting system. These not only direct people along the route but also identify the exits.

Emergency lighting equipment must direct most of the light downwards from a position normally above head height. This is to avoid high levels of luminaire brightness occurring in the normal areas of view, which could cause disability glare and in turn could hinder the evacuation process.

Although lifts will not form part of a designated escape route, it is essential to include emergency lighting in lift cars to provide some comfort to anyone trapped inside.

SHUT-DOWN LIGHTING AND STANDBY LIGHTING

In addition to providing escape lighting it may be necessary for the emergency system to provide illumination for operators to safely shut down hazardous or vital processes before they leave. Without this, further danger could arise both to the operators and to other users of the building.

In some situations, such as hospital operating theatres, it may be necessary to provide emergency lighting to allow normal activities to continue substantially unchanged. This is described as **emergency standby lighting**. It requires an alternative power supply, often of substantial capacity; a standby generator may be the answer, but the time required for the generator to reach full output needs to be considered.

EQUIPMENT AND SYSTEM DESIGN

Emergency lighting systems can be supplied from a central power supply or be self-contained. Central power systems can be either batteries fed from an automatic charger, or a central generator. Each requires its own dedicated and protected wiring installation. Self-contained systems use luminaires that incorporate their own battery power supplies. Each also contains a charger and a change-over device to switch the lamp on automatically when the main supply fails.

Luminaires can be self-contained fittings, which operate only when the normal supply fails, or can be normal luminaires that also incorporate a lamp and other components for emergency lighting purposes. The second option may be preferred by the architect or client, as it avoids a further piece of equipment to be fixed to the walls or ceiling.

Emergency lighting equipment needs to be of high quality to ensure that it will operate successfully when required. To ensure this there are, in many countries, national standards covering both the specification of the equipment and the design of the system as a whole. These are intended to ensure that adequate illumination is provided throughout a designated period of operation. It is essential to ensure the continuing reliability of a system by regular maintenance and testing, and by recording tests in a log book.

This chapter has given only an overall description of emergency lighting. It is a very important topic, because people's lives can depend on it. Current standards should be consulted, and any emergency lighting system that is provided should meet at least these minimum requirements. In the UK, British and European standards apply. It is also necessary to consult enforcing authorities (such as fire-fighting services) to ensure that any local requirements are met.

Maintenance, energy and costs

14

Much of the earlier material has dealt primarily with the design of the lit environment in a visual sense, but there are other important issues that the designer needs to consider for an installation to be successful, not just when new but throughout its life. This chapter discusses the following:

- **Lighting maintenance.** This topic is often overlooked by the designer. An installation can quickly deteriorate and cease to provide the quantities and qualities required unless an effective maintenance programme is incorporated.

- **Energy efficiency.** Lighting consumes a large percentage of the electric energy generated in many countries. Often this power is produced by burning fossil fuels – a finite resource, which eventually will be exhausted. Through this process large quantities of pollution are discharged into the atmosphere, causing damage to the environment on a global scale. It is the responsibility of all designers to ensure that energy is used efficiently and effectively.

- **Lighting costs.** People will always plump for the cheapest option that they believe will satisfy their need, often without fully understanding the lifetime cost of the installation. Capital and operating costs of lighting should be evaluated in the context of the total cost of constructing and running the building.

Other environmental issues that need to be considered at the design stage include the effect of lighting – both natural and electric – on other building services, particularly heating, ventilation and cooling. The eventual disposal of lighting equipment also needs to be considered not just by the designer, but by the building user and operator as well.

It is part of lighting design to balance these issues with the lighting requirements of the building and its users.

INSTALLATION MAINTENANCE

Lighting maintenance needs to be considered at two levels. The first is the cleaning and repair of the installation throughout its life, and the second is the effect of light loss due to the ageing of the installation.

Unless there is safe and easy access to lighting equipment, maintenance is neglected or expensive to implement, and the lighting deteriorates. This applies both to windows (cases exist of recent buildings where extensive glazing is neglected because the difficulty and cost of cleaning are prohibitive) and to luminaires. If long ladders or scaffolding are required, lamps are not replaced immediately after failure, and cleaning or repair is infrequent.

The client or the building manager needs to be informed about maintenance of the lighting equipment. Two aspects need to be covered:

- **The cleaning process**, noting especially detergents that will produce the best effect – those with anti-static properties to minimize the attraction of dust and dirt – and the use of non-abrasive cleaners to avoid damaging reflectors.
- **The frequency of cleaning.** This is determined by the type of application and the cleanliness of the surrounding environment. The quantity of atmospheric dirt can vary dramatically between a heavy engineering site in the centre of a busy city and a hospital set in the countryside.

The effectiveness of a lighting installation depends not only on the maintenance of the lighting equipment but also on the maintenance of room surfaces. Acting as secondary sources, these contribute to the interreflected light to a room and so need to be cleaned and regularly redecorated for lighting effectiveness to be continued.

Even with a planned and properly executed maintenance scheme the light output of an installation falls during the period between maintenance processes – the **maintenance cycle** of the installation. This deterioration is the result of dirt building up on light-emitting and reflecting surfaces. It also occurs because the light output of most lamps deteriorates through their life. Lamps eventually fail completely; in addition, some discharge lamps start to flicker towards the end of their life, which can be distracting and annoying and must be avoided.

The designer takes these effects into account by basing calculations on a **maintained illuminance**. This is the average illuminance over a particular surface at the end of the maintenance cycle: that is, at the point in time just before lamps are replaced or equipment and room surfaces are cleaned.

Choices of lamp and luminaire type, and the number used, are affected by maintenance conditions. The conditions are represented by a maintenance factor, which is incorporated in illuminance calculations. This is defined by

$$\text{maintenance factor (MF)} = \frac{\text{maintained illuminance}}{\text{initial illuminance}} \qquad (14.1)$$

It is the product of all the factors that affects the planned illuminance throughout the lifetime of the installation:

$$\text{MF} = \text{LLMF} \times \text{LSF} \times \text{LMF} \times \text{RSMF} \qquad (14.2)$$

where LLMF is the lamp lumen maintenance factor, LSF is the lamp survival factor, LMF is the luminaire maintenance factor, and RSMF is the room surface maintenance factor.

The lamp lumen maintenance factor takes account of the depreciation of lamp light output through life. The fall-off rate varies for different lamp types; the lamp manufacturer should be consulted for this information. The manufacturer should also provide information on lamp life and details of the lamp survival factor. This represents the fraction of lamp failures after a specific number of hours of operation with a typical switching cycle and supply voltage. It is used only when lamps are not to be replaced immediately when they fail (**spot lamp-replacement**).

The luminaire maintenance factor takes account of the dirt deposited on the optical surfaces of the luminaire. The rate of deterioration depends on the luminaire type and the extent to which dirt is present in the atmosphere. If the luminaire is sealed (that is, dust-proof or dust-tight), and with no upward light, dirt deposition is less of a problem than if the luminaire is open and has horizontal optical surfaces on which dust can accumulate. Luminaire manufacturers should be consulted about the likely maintenance factor. Table 14.1 gives typical values for luminaires that are cleaned annually.

The room surface maintenance factor takes account of the dirt accumulation on the light-reflecting surfaces of a room. This depends on the rate of the dirt deposition and the importance of interreflection to the illuminance produced. Interreflection depends in turn on room size and luminaire intensity distribution. For example, RSMF is less for a large room lit with luminaires that direct most of their light downwards than for a small room with indirect lighting. Table 14.2 shows typical values for two sizes of room and for direct flux luminaires (where most of the output reaches the reference plane directly), direct/indirect flux (a combination of direct illumination and light reaching the reference plane by reflection) and indirect flux (most of the light reaches the reference plane only after reflection).

Table 14.1 *Luminaire maintenance factors (LMF) for a cleaning interval of one year*

Luminaire type	Clean atmosphere	Normal atmosphere	Dirty atmosphere
Bare lamp batten	0.93	0.89	0.83
Open-top reflector	0.90	0.86	0.83
Closed-top reflector	0.89	0.81	0.72
Enclosed (IP2X)	0.88	0.82	0.77
Dustproof (IP5X)	0.94	0.90	0.86
Indirect uplighter	0.86	0.81	0.74

Table 14.2 *Room surface maintenance factors (RSMF) for a cleaning interval of one year*

(a) Small room: room index, K = 0.7

Luminaire flux distribution	Clean atmosphere	Normal atmosphere	Dirty atmosphere
Direct	0.97	0.94	0.93
Direct/indirect	0.90	0.86	0.82
Indirect	0.85	0.78	0.73

(b) Large room: room index, K = 5.0

Luminaire flux distribution	Clean atmosphere	Normal atmosphere	Dirty atmosphere
Direct	0.98	0.96	0.95
Direct/indirect	0.92	0.88	0.85
Indirect	0.88	0.82	0.77

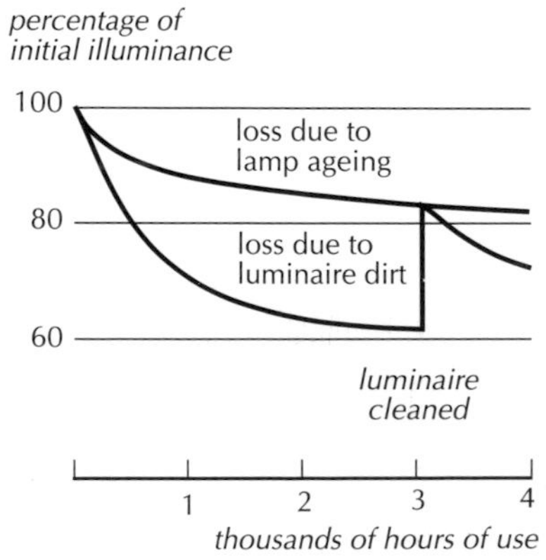

Figure 14.1 *Typical light loss due to lamp ageing and luminaire dirt.*

Figure 14.1 shows how light loss due to lamp ageing (LLMF) and to luminaire dirt accumulation (LMF) increases with time during the maintenance cycle.

Using the maintenance factor approach to design means providing a higher-than-required illuminance when the installation is new. This is to ensure that the maintained illuminance is achieved at the end of the maintenance cycle. The initial over-provision can be overcome by using luminaires with dimmer control together with a light sensor that monitors the illuminance and keeps it at the required value. The light output will be turned down at the start of the maintenance cycle but will be on fully at the end. The initial cost of the installation is greater, but it can be a cost-effective solution as a result of energy saving.

At the costing stages of design, the client should be informed about the maintenance procedure required for high-quality lighting throughout the life of the installation, and also the maintenance factor values on which the design is based. This enables the client to compare different design solutions on an equal basis.

Electric lighting maintenance is sometimes carried out by specialist companies, which clean and repair luminaires and carry out lamp replacement. The lamp replacement can be either spot replacement or block replacement at set times in the life of the installation, when cleaning is done. These companies can also arrange for the disposal of lamps and luminaires at the end of their life. Lamps and luminaires sometimes incorporate materials that could be harmful to the environment, and need special processes for their disposal.

Dirt on glazing reduces the quantity of daylight entering a room. Maintenance factors in daylight calculations, like those for electric lighting, take into account the cleaning frequency and the atmospheric quality. Window dirt deposition depends also on the tilt of the glazing: vertical windows receive less dirt than rooflights and are more efficiently washed by rain. Table 14.3 gives typical values adopted for daylight estimation; in very dirty industrial atmospheres where windows receive little maintenance the values can be even lower than those shown.

Table 14.3 *Typical maintenance factors adopted in daylighting calculations*

Angle of glazing	Clean atmosphere	Urban atmosphere	Industrial atmosphere
Vertical	0.9	0.8	0.7
Sloping	0.8	0.7	0.6
Horizontal	0.7	0.6	0.5

The designer has a responsibility for site safety: the design and specification of an installation must be such that it can be constructed, maintained and eventually dismantled and disposed of without hazard. This is a moral responsibility, and it is often a legal duty (as under the Construction, Design and Maintenance Regulations in the UK). In practice it constrains the placing of windows and luminaires to positions where access during their lifetime is reasonable, considering the normal use of the building. If, alternatively, there is not safe access to any element for maintenance then loss of performance by dirt or lamp failure must be explicitly taken into account during design, and this must be made clear to building users.

ENERGY EFFICIENCY IN LIGHTING

Energy efficiency is important for two reasons. First, it reduces operating costs for the client; second (and more important) it reduces the consumption of the world's stock of fossil fuels – coal, oil and natural gas. Fossil fuels provide the primary energy for generating the bulk of electricity in many countries, but this process causes pollution by discharge of carbon dioxide into the atmosphere, contributing to climate changes and to acid rain – both detrimental to the environment on a global scale. In 1992, in Rio de Janeiro, members of the United Nations agreed to reduce the emission of greenhouse gases to the 1990 level by the year 2000. In 1997 members of the European Commission agreed to further reductions, and Britain agreed to reduce emissions further by the year 2010.

In the UK, in 1994, it was estimated that lighting used around 17% of the total energy consumption of commercial and public buildings. However, because this was entirely through the use of electricity, it created around 26% of the CO_2 emission. It is therefore vital to include energy efficiency in any lighting design. This means considering the equipment used, the installation design, and how it is used.

Considering the lighting equipment, it is necessary to ensure efficient conversion of electricity into light, by selecting lamps that are appropriate for the purpose and have a high efficacy. Usually this means using discharge lamps that have efficacies of at least 50 lm/W. If colour rendering is unimportant then low-pressure sodium lamps can be used, which have an efficacy of up to 200 lm/W. The incandescent lamp, however, has an efficacy of around 12 lm/W: considerably lower than any discharge source. There will still be good reasons for their use in some situations; then, if possible, low-voltage tungsten–halogen sources should be used, which have efficacies of around 15 lm/W. But in many situations where an incandescent lamp has been used in the past, compact fluorescent lamps can now be used. Table 4.1 in Chapter 4 shows the typical efficacy of a range of lamps.

It is also important to use luminaires that emit a high proportion of the lamp light output, and which direct the light to where it is required. This implies the use of luminaires that have a high light output ratio and an appropriate intensity distribution. Efficiency can be assessed by a luminaire's utilization factor, although this applies only when fittings are used in a regular array.

For a high light output, the luminaire designer has to provide an efficient optical system, using highly reflective materials, and efficient control gear. Modern control gear for discharge lamps uses high-frequency operation, which can improve the efficiency by 20% compared with a wire-wound choke. It also enables dimming which can provide additional savings. High-frequency lamp operation has a further advantage of imperceptible flicker, which leads to improved human comfort and in some cases a lower incidence of headaches.

Installation design for good energy use begins by ensuring that lighting is not spread unnecessarily. For example, much lighting in commercial buildings has in the past been provided by regular arrays of ceiling-mounted luminaires, giving uniform illuminance over the horizontal working plane. This means that tasks may be accommodated anywhere in the space. If, however, a lower illuminance can be provided between task areas, perhaps over circulation routes, then savings are made. This type of design is sometimes referred to as **task and background** lighting or, more recently, **task and building** lighting. It requires considerable care to ensure an appropriate design for all requirements, but energy savings of up to 40% have been estimated. A further benefit of this approach is that it provides a non-uniform distribution of light, which research shows may be preferred by users. However, as we have seen in Chapter 7, it can be important to ensure that room surfaces, particular the walls and ceilings, have an appearance of lightness.

Energy efficiency is dependent also on the control systems of electric lighting and on how they are used. Lighting is often left on when it is not required – when there is adequate daylight or when the space is unoccupied. People tend to switch lights on when they are first needed, such as early on a dark winter morning, but neglect to switch them off again as daylight increases. It is not unusual for electric lighting to remain on all day, until the last person leaves. This is found particularly in shared rooms, or in spaces such as circulation areas where no one person is responsible.

Electric lighting can be controlled automatically by using timers, light sensors and occupancy sensors to switch or to dim luminaires so that the designed illumination is maintained. However, people dislike being dictated to, so any control system must be unobtrusive and user-friendly. A commonly used system allows people to switch lights on, but turns them off automatically when daylight illuminance is adequate; but the controls must incorporate a manual override.

Energy efficiency is the subject of legislation in many countries. For instance, the Approved Document of Part L of the UK Building Regulations 1995 stipulates that for modern installations 95% of the installed lighting circuit watts must be based on the use of fluorescent, metal halide, high-pressure sodium or induction lamps. An alternative method of complying is to have an average efficacy for the whole installation of not less than 50 lumens per circuit watt. However, some display-type installations can be exempt. Lighting controls also form part of the regulations, and specification is given about the maximum distance that a manual switch should be from the luminaires it controls.

Lighting controls can provide user benefits as well as energy efficiency. These benefits include the opportunity to change lighting for different tasks or applications, or to alter the lighting to suit a different room layout without the need to physically change the installation. Luminaires can be switched remotely via a building management system (BMS), and can be operated by users with hand-held controllers similar to those used to operate televisions and video recorders. Lighting can also be controlled via telephone or computer networks, giving considerable flexibility.

Controls systems are a rapidly developing area of technology, and the designer is advised to seek current information from professional institutions and specialist manufacturers.

LIGHTING COSTS: CAPITAL AND OPERATIONAL

The costs of providing lighting need to be examined in three categories: capital expenditure, operating expenditure and the effect of lighting on productivity.

- **Capital expenditure.** For electric lighting this includes the cost of the design, the equipment (lamps, luminaires and controls), the installation (wiring, fixing and installing the luminaires and controls), any associated builders' work, and the commissioning of the installation (adjusting and testing). On average this represents approximately 5% of the total building costs for a commercial building. The capital expenditure of daylighting is the cost of windows in comparison with the cost of the equivalent area of solid wall or roof, the costs of any particular building form, site use or orientation required to make the good use of skylight or sunlight, and any costs associated with special room planning. A cost associated with achieving deep skylight penetration is an increase in ceiling height from that required on all other considerations.
- **Lighting operating cost.** Energy, cleaning and replacement (as described earlier) are the main continuing outlays with electric lighting. With daylighting there are two groups of running costs: cleaning and repair, and the energy costs of the other

environmental effects of windows. Increased window sizes can create the need for both additional heating in winter and additional cooling when excessive solar gain occurs.

- **User's productivity.** Good lighting can enhance performance both directly, by providing an appropriate illumination in a glare-free environment, and indirectly, by providing lighting that raises the feeling of well-being – which in turn enhances performance. Typically, in a commercial building, the lighting operating costs are approximately 5% of the running costs whereas the salary cost of the workforce may be 80% of the total. Savings in the cost of the lighting that adversely affect performance are a false economy.

The cost analysis of a lighting installation needs to be done in terms of life cycle costing, considering both capital and operating costs for the expected life of the installation. A system that is initially cheap, such as the use of incandescent lamps in a factory area, is usually much more expensive over its lifetime than one with higher capital costs but significantly better efficacy and longer lamp life, such as an installation using high-pressure discharge lamps.

Windows and electric lighting have effects on the general environmental performance of a building. Table 14.4 gives a design checklist of these. It can be seen that lighting cannot be considered in isolation, either in terms of cost or in its implications for the design of the building structure and its various services installations. An important point is that interactions between lighting and thermal factors affect the relative costs of daylight and electric lighting over the lifetime of the building. A high level of daylight requires large windows and high ceilings; there can be significant variation in indoor temperature and discomfort due to other thermal effects of the windows; and heating and cooling energy costs can be high. Conversely, the use of full electric lighting during daylight hours, with windows only where necessary for view, ignores the contribution to energy saving that can be gained from natural lighting, and loses the variability that is a stimulus to occupant well-being.

Most research studies have shown that, in general, the optimum balance of daylighting and electric lighting is found when

- the area of glazing is sufficiently great to make a significant contribution to interior lighting;
- there is supplementary well-controlled electric lighting during daylight hours.

The supplementary lighting must be designed specifically to respond to changes in available daylight. The topic is discussed also in the last section of Chapter 10.

When alternative designs are compared – based on maintaining a specific interior illuminance with different combinations of window size and electric lighting – U-shaped curves are found on the graph of cost against glazed area. Lifetime cost is higher with very large or very small windows, and there is a fairly flat intermediate region that represents minimum costs. A similar conclusion is reached when lifetime energy use rather than lifetime financial cost is examined, and guidelines for occupant satisfaction suggest a similar conclusion.

Table 14.4   *Checklist of other environmental factors*

Heat gain
Is the energy use of electric lighting minimized?
Is heat from luminaires dispersed efficiently?
Are windows shaded or of heat-rejecting glazing to minimize excessive solar gain?
Is solar gain employed usefully where heating is required?

Heat loss
Is the insulation value of glazing sufficient
– to minimize energy loss?
– to avoid cold interior surfaces?

Ventilation
Is natural ventilation required?
Are the windows sealed adequately to avoid unwanted air infiltration?

Noise
Is there external noise that
– constrains choice of window positions?
– prevents window opening?
– requires the window to have high acoustic insulation?

Other building services
Is wiring to luminaires compatible with other wired services, such as communications?
Do luminaires interfere with ducts or air-handling equipment?
Is space available for lighting control systems?

Safety and sustainability
Can the installation be installed and maintained safely?
Do lamps or luminaires contain materials harmful to the environment?
Can they be recycled or disposed of safely?

Part Three

Calculations

What calculations are for

15

Calculations are not an end in themselves. Their purpose is to help the designer to choose between alternatives or to check whether a particular solution meets a criterion. They are a small part of the whole design process – an aid to creativity in lighting, not a substitute.

USE AND ACCURACY

There are many methods available for estimating each of the quantities that a lighting designer needs to know. None is ideal for all circumstances: they vary in accuracy, in generality, and in cost (and there is the underlying rule that the more information that can be gained from a computation, and the more precise the output, the greater the costs of time and resources). Our needs as designers also vary – from one job to another and, particularly, from stage to stage of the design process.

The first stage of a scheme involves decisions about the overall form of the building, its orientation and the choice of major materials. There is the need to check the implications of alternative basic forms, to make rapid calculations of sunlight and daylight in relation to site planning, and to assess strategies of energy use. Calculations at this stage can embody only initial assumptions about construction and materials; they are concerned with overall quantities of light rather than prediction of specific performance, and they often need to be applied to many alternative designs. The first category of calculation is therefore that of procedures that can be used for generating forms – for setting limits or giving basic dimensions.

The second category are those usually applied at the stage of detailed design, when underlying parameters have been fixed. The needs are to find precise dimensions or numbers. Calculations are necessary to confirm that specific criteria are satisfied or to select, for example, the particular types of luminaire and lamp to be used. They may also be used in the design of control systems and in investigating the distribution of daylight within a space so that daytime electric lighting can be planned.

The third category of calculations are those needed for presentation. The output may be entirely visual – the production of rendered images – or may be a numerical demonstration of scheme performance.

In every case, accuracy is governed by the precision of the assumptions made in a calculation. Lighting is much affected by factors such as surface dirt and by the actual furnishings and finishes of a room – and, with daylighting, by exterior obstructions due to trees and other buildings. There is always uncertainty in the values entered into an equation, and the results of calculations must be interpreted accordingly. It is nonsense, in general practice, to compute electric lighting to fractions of a lux, or daylight to several decimal places of daylight factor. If a maintenance factor or a room surface reflectance is only an educated guess, no number computed from this can be more precise.

Nor, usually, does it need to be: small changes of illuminance have little meaning within the total sensitivity range of the eye. We have seen that minor variation is often imperceptible and without effect on visual performance, and that it is insignificant in comparison with the natural variation of daylight. It is only in comparing schemes for contractual purposes or in checking against formal (but arbitrary) standards that apparently exact calculated numbers become important in practice.

The need for interpretative care applies not only to results from simple manual procedures. Computer programs for lighting prediction vary in their calculation methods from automation of simple manual methods to procedures using radiosity or ray-tracing algorithms. The inherent accuracy of the method used is not always clear from the presentation of the software; and there always remains the overriding constraint determined by uncertainty in the input data. There is a special risk, in using computer calculations, of assuming a greater accuracy than can be justified. Lighting within a room is a complex, varying quantity, and most calculations are based on very simplified models of reality, with input data that are mere estimates.

STANDARDS AND DATA

The working references for the designer in practice are the publications of national professional institutions, such as the *Code for Interior Lighting* published by the Chartered Institution of Building

Services Engineers in the United Kingdom and the *Lighting Handbook* of the Illuminating Engineering Society of North America. These in turn refer to national standards and legislation covering particular building types – with which the designer must, of course, be familiar. It is also important that up-to-date manufacturers' data are used when selecting materials and equipment, and that, where available, local climatic information is used when assessing daylighting and energy use.

There is much in common between different national lighting codes, so the tables in this book summarize frequently used criteria and some of the technical data of lamps, luminaires and daylight. As well as giving data for example calculations, the aim is to provide a series of checklists for requirements that may lie in particular codes and standards.

Examples

16

This chapter illustrates some frequently used calculation methods, setting the steps involved in each and showing where judgement is necessary in the use of the results. Often in real schemes there are conflicting requirements, and compromise or a choice out of several not-quite-perfect solutions is necessary.

The examples are set out in a standard format: each begins with a short description of the purpose; then the steps of the method, with any equations and symbols, are listed; the example calculation itself follows; and finally there are comments.

All the methods given are for hand calculation, although a few can be programmed easily as computer spreadsheets. In some cases, computer methods are quicker than the procedures shown, especially where several alternative designs have to be evaluated, but in general the approaches are similar. The data used are selected from the sheets given in Section (i); in practice, of course, manufacturers' current data and site-specific information should be applied.

The examples are derived from actual buildings. The first five consider different aspects of lighting in the same room, a secretarial office on the ground floor of a nineteenth-century building. Shown in Figure 16.1, it has three large windows, which face approximately west (255° from north) with a view over level open ground to another building, which is flat-roofed and 60 m away. An extension to this building is proposed: a new wing extending forward at the same roof height, and reducing the daylight in the office being studied. The proposed extension is shown in outline on the site plan.

The following pages examine daylight falling on the office windows, the general level of natural light in the room, the number of luminaires required for general electric lighting, and the use of electric lighting in conjunction with daylight.

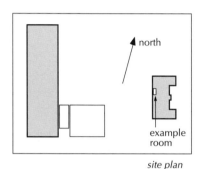

section

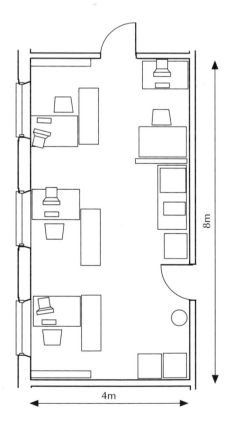

site plan

Figure 16.1 *Example building.*

(a) VERTICAL SKY COMPONENT AND SITE LAYOUT

Purpose

This calculation is used mainly at the early design stage of a project, when the overall block form is considered and overshadowing might be a problem. It can also be used to evaluate the likely effect of a new obstruction at an existing window.

A commonly used criterion for assessing the likely effect of a new building on existing daylighting is given in *Site layout planning for daylight and sunlight: a guide to good practice* (Building Research Establishment, 1991):

> *The skylight (diffuse daylight) of an existing building may be judged to be adversely affected if 'the vertical sky component measured at the centre of an existing main window is less than 27%, and less than 0.8 times its former value'.*

The vertical sky component (D_{sv}) is described in Chapter 5. If the block layout of a new scheme is being tested, the window positions may not be known; then D_{sv} is calculated at appropriate points 2 m above ground level on the building facade.

Method

Rule of thumb:

> D_{sv} is 27% when there is a continuous horizontal obstruction giving a skyline 25° above the horizon.

It follows that if no part of an obstruction subtends an elevation greater than 25° from the reference point, the criterion given above is satisfied.

If the skyline is uneven, with part higher than 25° and part lower, D_{sv} may still be more than 27%, but this needs to be calculated. The method involves plotting an outline of the obstructions on a stereographic drawing and then superimposing a D_{sv} dot diagram. The two steps are as follows:

1 Find the azimuth and angle of elevation of each point on the skyline as seen from the reference point (the position being studied on the affected building). This is normally the centre of a window opening.

   The azimuth, α, is most easily measured from a site plan, and is taken clockwise from north. The elevation angle, γ, is found from the difference in height, h, between the reference point and the skyline point, and the plan distance, d. Then

$$\gamma = \arctan\left(\frac{h}{d}\right) \tag{16.1}$$

(The inverse tangent, **arctan**, is sometimes marked tan⁻¹ on calculator keyboards.)

Plot the skyline (and any other obstructions) on the stereographic base, given in Section (i), page 156. On a stereographic diagram a horizontal edge appears as a curved line, so with a long skyline it is necessary to find an intermediate point to draw the arc accurately. The stereographic projection of a horizontal line is sometimes called a **droop line**, and publications that give sunpath diagrams often include an overlay of droop lines for tracing.

2 Superimpose as an overlay the D_{sv} dot diagram, page 156. It should be rotated to face the direction of view at the reference point: that is, the azimuth perpendicular to the window wall.

There are 158 V-points on the diagram. Count the number, n, that are obscured by the obstructions. The vertical sky component at the reference point is then

$$D_{sv} = \frac{158 - n}{4}\% \tag{16.2}$$

This should be rounded to the nearest whole number.

Example

Figure 16.2 shows the building and its site. The first calculation studies the daylight available on the face of the middle window in the office, at the centre of the opening.

The skyline of the building directly opposite makes an angle of approximately 18° above the horizon. Using the rule of thumb, it is clear that the existing building would not cause D_{sv} to fall below 27%. The new wing, however, projects forward, and its skyline would be higher than 25°: therefore a more detailed calculation is necessary.

Figure 16.2 has the relevant corners of the obstructing building labelled A to E, and Table 16.1 shows how the azimuth and elevation of each corner can be calculated for the reference point. The distances and azimuth angles are measured from the site plan, and the elevation angles are based on a height difference of 20 m between skyline and reference point. In Figure 16.3 the skyline corners are plotted on the stereographic base.

Figure 16.4 shows the vertical sky component dots diagram superimposed, rotated 255° clockwise from north (to give the orientation

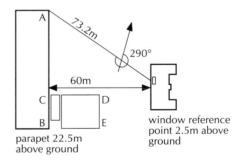

Figure 16.2 *Distances and angles for calculating obstruction to daylight.*

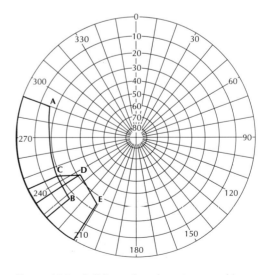

Figure 16.3 *Buildings plotted on stereographic diagram.*

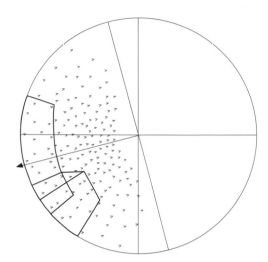

Figure 16.4 *Vertical sky component dots super-imposed. The arrow points towards the orientation of the window wall, 255° clockwise from north.*

Table 16.1 *Plan distance, d, between window reference and skyline points; azimuth, α, and elevation, γ, of skyline points*

Point	d (metres)	α (degrees from north)	γ (degrees above horizon)
A	73.2	290	arctan (20/73.2) = 15.3
B	66.6	229	16.7
C	60.7	246	18.2
D	31.3	237	32.6
E	41.7	211	25.6

of the window wall). There are 24 dots enclosed by the outline of the original obstructing building, each representing $0.25D_{sv}$. The proposed extension encloses another 11 dots. Using equation (16.2), the corresponding sky components on the vertical reference point are therefore

$$D_{sv} \text{ (original)} = \frac{158-24}{4} = 33.5 \approx 34\%$$

$$D_{sv} \text{ (with proposed extension)} = \frac{158-35}{4} = 30.75\% \approx 31\%$$

Comment

The new obstruction reduces the available daylight by about one-tenth. The value of D_{sv} remains greater than 27%, so the effect of the obstruction on diffuse daylight in the office would normally be considered insignificant. Under the variability of real sky conditions, the difference would probably be not detectable on site in short-term measurements.

However, an insignificant drop in skylight does not mean that the occupants of a building would be insensitive to an increased obstruction. In general, such factors as a loss of view and a perception of reduced privacy can trigger strong responses. This is especially the case where the affected building is a house. Daylight is more easily quantified than, for example, view or privacy: therefore it is often used as the core of an argument against a new building project, although the main objections may be subjective, and dependent on many factors.

In English law, reference to **rights to light** gives a way in which obstruction to a long-established opening to the sky can be challenged. The criteria used are derived from daylighting concepts current in the 1920s, and have little relationship with current lighting practice, but they form part of a mechanism for determining legal damages.

Diagrams based on the gnomonic projection provide an alternative method of calculating vertical sky components. They can be simpler to plot, but are often less accurate than the stereographic diagrams given here. Examples are to be found in *Site layout planning for daylight and sunlight: a guide to good practice* (Building Research Establishment, 1991).

(b) SUNLIGHT AVAILABILITY

Purpose

The incidence of direct sunlight may need to be checked, either because it is desirable for warmth or for illumination, or because it is unwanted and would cause overheating and glare. Some of the criteria are discussed in the section on sunlight in Chapter 10.

Method

The stereographic projection employed for vertical sky component calculations can be used directly for assessing sunlight. These are the steps:

1   As in step 1 of the previous calculation, plot on the stereographic base the outline of obstructions seen from the point under study, the reference point. If this is within a room, the outline of a window opening can be constructed by the same method, finding the azimuth and elevation of the opening's corners from the reference point.

2   To find probable sunlight hours (as described in Chapters 5 and 7), superimpose a T_{ps} diagram. The diagram for London is given in section (i), page 157. Each cross on the diagram represents 0.5% of probable annual sunshine hours: that is, if the centres of n crosses are visible above obstructions, sunlight would fall on the reference point for the following percentage of the time it is shining on unobstructed ground:

$$T_{ps} = \frac{n}{2}\%$$
(16.3)

Similarly, if an obstruction screens *m* crosses from view, it reduces the probable sunlight hours by *m*/2 percentage hours.

The curved line is the equinox sunpath (approximately 21 March and 23 September). This permits the available sunlight in the summer and winter semesters to be found separately.

3　To find the actual times when the sun could be visible from the reference point, superimpose a sunpath diagram on the obstruction outline. A sunpath diagram for London is given in section (i), page 157.

It must be remembered that sunpath diagrams usually are plotted for **solar time**, which may differ from clock time, so the effects of longitude differences or of national time regulations (such as daylight saving or summer time) must be considered. These are discussed in Chapter 5. In addition, the equation of time can give errors of about quarter of an hour.

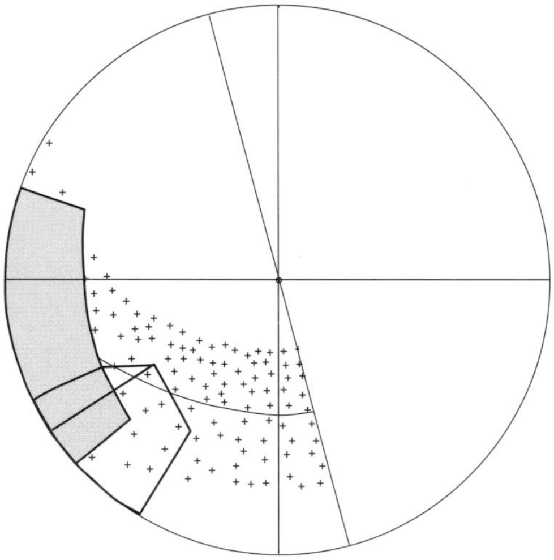

Example

This continues the previous example to find the effect that the proposed extension to the obstructing building has on sunlight availability.

In Figure 16.5 the T_{ps} diagram for London is laid over the outline of the obstruction. The sloping line across the diagram represents the window wall (the line gives its orientation in plan). It shows how the wall itself screens half of the sky from a reference point on its surface.

Counting the crosses, it is found that there are 103 with centres lying outside the original obstruction, so the sun would on average be visible from the face of the window wall for 51.5% of the time that sunlight would fall on unobstructed ground. The centres of 11 crosses lie within the outline of the proposed extension: therefore this would further reduce sunlight availability to 46%.

Sunlight within a room can be found by drawing the outlines of window openings; the procedure for plotting these is exactly the same as given for external obstructions. Figure 16.6 is an example. Here the window outlines are shown for a reference point that is on a desk surface 1 m back from the centre window. These window outlines are overlaid first on the external obstructions and then on the sunpath diagram; they show how the sky is masked from the new reference point.

Comparing this with the original sunpath diagram on page 157, it can be seen that sunlight coming from the centre window could fall on the desk surface from just before 2 pm in June until after 6 pm. The new extension would block the short period of sunshine that at present comes through the window during the winter months.

Figure 16.5 *Probable sunlight hours diagram superimposed.*

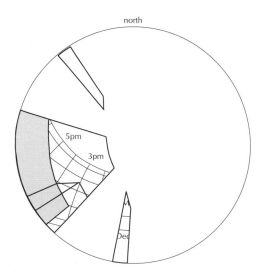

Figure 16.6 *Window openings and obstructions over sunpath diagram.*

No sunlight reaches the reference point from the more northerly window. The southerly window allows a few minutes of low-altitude sunlight to sweep across the reference point in winter.

Comment

In a residential building or in the circulation area of a public building, sunlight might be desirable. Then the relatively small drop in the percentage of probable sunlight hours would show that the proposed extension would still leave sufficient available sunlight, by the criteria discussed in Chapter 9. However, because the room being studied is a secretarial office, sunlight penetration is likely to cause nuisance and discomfort: therefore shading of some kind is necessary. If internal blinds are provided, occupants would tend to close them on sunny afternoons. This could affect the daylighting in the room and hence the use of electric lighting.

Graphical methods for predicting sunlight in buildings can be slow and cumbersome. Computer programs, particularly those linked with standard CAD packages, are quicker for illustrating sunshine and shadow patterns; but most convenient in the early design stages of a scheme is the use of block models with a heliodon. If a heliodon is not available, a light source and a model sundial can be used. The source can be the actual sun, or a small lamp held sufficiently far from the model to minimize the effect of the non-parallel beam.

(c) AVERAGE DAYLIGHT FACTOR: PLANNING FOR DAYLIGHT

Purpose

The average daylight factor ($\overline{D}$) is used to predict the extent to which daylighting will be a significant factor in the lighting of a room. It applies to cloudy climates where skylight (as opposed to reflected sunlight) is employed as the main source of natural light. It is particularly useful for finding the overall area of glazing required at the early design stages of a project.

Design criteria are discussed in Chapter 9. In summary: if $\overline{D}$ is less than 2% then electric lighting is likely to be needed in the room during daytime hours, and will appear dominant; between 2% and 5%, supplementary lighting may be needed during daytime but the room will appear to be daylit; above 5%, electric lighting will not normally be necessary but thermal problems become increasingly likely.

Method

The average daylight factor is the mean daylight factor on the horizontal working plane. It is given by the following equation:

$$\overline{D} = \frac{A_\text{g}}{A} \frac{\theta \tau}{\left(1 - \rho^2\right)} \tag{16.4}$$

When there are several windows, with different glazing or different angles of external obstruction, $\overline{D}$ is calculated for each window separately, and the results are added together. If the windows have similar characteristics the daylight factor can be calculated from the total glazed area.

The symbols in equation (16.4) have the following meanings:

A_g Glazed area of windows (not including window frames, glazing bars or other obstructions).

A Total area of enclosing room surfaces (ceiling, floor, walls including windows).

θ Angle of visible sky, measured in section from a reference point in the centre of the window opening in the plane of the inside window wall (see Figure 16.7).

τ Transmittance of glazing to diffuse light, including the effect of dirt. The diffuse transmittance of clear single glazing is approximately 0.8, clear double glazing approximately 0.7. Typical maintenance factors are given in Chapter 14, Table 14.3 and glass transmittances in section (i).

ρ Mean reflectance of enclosing room surfaces. During design, this can often be only an educated guess; typical values are 0.5 for a room with white ceiling and light-coloured walls, 0.3 for a normal office or living room. Page 159 contains a list of typical reflectances.

When the method is used at the early design stage to find the area of glazing needed in a room to give a particular average daylight factor, the equation is inverted:

$$A_\text{g} = \frac{\overline{D} A \left(1 - \rho^2\right)}{\theta \tau} \tag{16.5}$$

The main equation, (16.4), is valid only when the external obstruction gives a horizontal skyline. If the skyline is uneven but the mean height of the obstructions is approximately constant across the

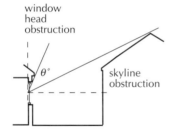

window head obstruction

$\theta°$

skyline obstruction

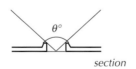

$\theta°$

section

Figure 16.7 *Sky angle, θ, for a side window and a rooflight. The reference point is the centre of the window opening on the plane of the inside surface.*

skyline, this mean height makes an acceptable approximation. In other cases, such as where a window looks into a courtyard, a different form of the equation can be used:

$$\overline{D} = \frac{A_g}{A} \frac{2\,D_{sv}\,\tau}{\left(1-\rho^2\right)} \tag{16.6}$$

where D_{sv} is the vertical sky component on the outside window wall, calculated as in section (a) above. In this equation an approximation is made by balancing the light reflected onto the window by the ground and external obstructions against skylight screened by the window head.

Example

This calculation finds the mean daylight factor in the office illustrated in Figure 16.1, initially with only the original obstructing building. Assume that the internal reflectances are: ceiling 0.7, wall surfaces 0.4, floor 0.2.

A_g	Glazed area	6.9 m^2
	3 windows, each 2.2 m high, 1.3 m wide overall, assuming 20% of total area is obstructed by frame and glazing bars	
A	Area of enclosing room surfaces	136 m^2
	Ceiling (32 m^2) + walls and windows (72 m^2) + floor (32 m^2)	
θ	Angle of visible sky	57°
	Measured in section: 90° − 15° (window head) − 18° (obstructing building)	
τ	Transmittance of glazing	0.64
	0.8 (diffuse transmittance of single glazing) × 0.8 (maintenance factor)	
ρ	Mean reflectance of room surfaces	0.41
	based on reflectance of ceiling, 0.7; vertical surfaces excluding windows, 0.4; window glazing, 0.1; floor, 0.2	

The room reflectance is an area-weighted mean. That is, each surface area is multiplied by the corresponding reflectance, and the total of these is then divided by the total area:

$$\frac{32 \times 0.7 + 65.1 \times 0.4 + 6.9 \times 0.1 + 32 \times 0.2}{136} = 0.408$$

Then, using equation (16.4):

$$\overline{D} = \frac{6.9 \times 57 \times 0.64}{136 \times (1 - 0.41^2)} = 2.225\%$$
$$\approx 2\%$$

The method in its alternative form (equation (16.6)) makes it possible to compare the original obstruction with the total shading caused by the new obstruction. We use the vertical sky components calculated in section (a) above:

D_{sv} Vertical sky component   with existing building   33.5%

                                          with proposed extension   30.75%

Then:

$$\overline{D} \text{ (original obstruction)} = \frac{6.9 \times 2 \times 33.5 \times 0.64}{136 \times (1 - 0.41^2)} \approx 2.6\%$$

$$\overline{D} \text{ (with new extension)} = \frac{6.9 \times 2 \times 30.75 \times 0.64}{136 \times (1 - 0.41^2)} \approx 2.4\%$$

Comment

The average daylight factor of about 2% indicates that the room may be perceived as a daylit room, but supplementary electric lighting will probably be needed during daylight hours.

It is not surprising that equations (16.4) and (16.6) give differing results. The first equation assumes a continuous obstruction, while the actual obstructing building does not stretch across the horizon, and allows some light to reach the window from either end. But the equations are both approximations on differing bases, and there would be a small discrepancy in the results even if the length of the obstruction were to be taken into account.

This illustrates the care that must be taken in interpreting lighting calculations. The daylight factor method is very useful in predicting the nature of the lit environment of a room, but in taking into account the accuracy of the criteria used and the assumptions in the calculation, $\overline{D}$ should not normally be expressed to more precision than the nearest whole number. The average daylight factor is a good indicator of overall daylight quantity, but in the simple form given here it is not an exact measure. Where calculations are made to examine, for instance, the effect of new obstructions, the types of equation used and the parameters adopted must be matched. On these grounds we can see from the final calculation above that the daylight inside the room would be reduced by about a tenth if the new extension were built – probably an insignificant drop.

The daylight factor at a specific point in a room can be calculated in several ways. A good manual method is given in Building Research Establishment Digests 309 and 310, *Estimating daylight in buildings*. However, where daylight at several points needs to be studied, computer calculations are preferable (though not necessarily more accurate): illustrative contours of the daylight distribution can be displayed, and parameters can be changed easily to explore the effects of different window configurations or surface reflectances. Figure 16.8 shows contours of equal daylight factor in the example room.

(d) THE LUMEN METHOD: GENERAL ROOM LIGHTING

Purpose

A basic and commonly used approach to electric lighting design is to provide a nearly uniform illuminance across the working plane (which is usually taken to be horizontal). The aim is either to provide satisfactory working illumination for a particular type of task anywhere across the working plane or to give background illumination, which can be supplemented by local accent or task lighting where required.

The installation comprises a regular array of ceiling-mounted luminaires, either recessed, surface mounted or suspended from the ceiling. The choice of luminaire is determined by the required brightness pattern of the interior, the degree of glare control necessary for the application, and the lamp type required; see Chapters 4, 7 and 9.

The number of luminaires required depends on the planned horizontal plane illuminance, the total lamp light output of a single luminaire, and the proportion of this that will reach the working plane (either directly or by interreflection) – the **luminaire utilization factor** (*UF*). A further factor that needs to be taken into account is the decrease in light throughout the life of the installation – the **maintenance factor** (*MF*). This takes account of the lamp lumen depreciation as well as the depreciation of light due to dirt accumulation on the luminaire and room surfaces; see Chapter 14.

The lumen method is introduced in Chapter 1.

Method

1 Calculate the room index, *K*. This describes the proportions of a rectangular room:

$$K = \frac{LW}{(L+W)h_{\mathrm{m}}} \tag{16.7}$$

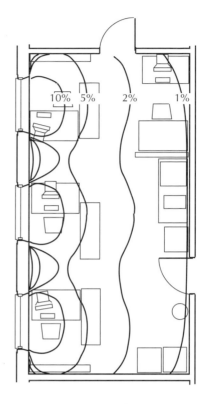

Figure 16.8 *Daylight factor contours in example office.*

where L is the length of the room and W is the width of the room; h_m is the height of the luminaire plane above the horizontal reference or working plane. If the luminaires are recessed into or are fixed onto the ceiling, h_m is the distance between the ceiling plane and the horizontal working plane; if the fittings are suspended, h_m is the distance between a horizontal plane passing through the centre-line of the luminaires and the horizontal working plane.

2 Calculate ceiling, wall and floor surface reflectances. These are area-weighted mean reflectances, as used in example (c) above. If the calculation is being made for a horizontal plane above the floor – for example a working plane at desk level – then the effective reflectance of that plane has to be used. An estimate is usually taken, based primarily on the floor reflectance. However, the actual fraction of light effectively reflected upwards from the level of the working plane depends on the proportions of the room below the plane, and on the lower wall and floor surface reflectances. It is lower than the area-weighted mean reflectance of these surface, and is termed a **cavity reflectance**. The reflectance of desktops at the working plane may also be taken into account.

3 Find the utilization factor for the luminaires to be used. This depends on the luminaire average luminous intensity distribution, the dimensions of the room, and the average reflectance of the main room surfaces. Although a lighting designer can calculate the UF for a particular situation, this information is usually provided by the luminaire manufacturer for a range of standard rectangular room configurations. Interpolation can be used for other rooms. Section (i), page 160 shows a typical presentation of utilization factor data and associated performance information for a twin fluorescent lamp luminaire with a system of louvres and reflectors to control the light output.

The luminaire performance table also includes a value for the nominal spacing-to-height ratio (SHR_{nom}). This is the maximum distance between luminaire centres at which a nearly uniform illuminance distribution is achieved across a horizontal reference or working plane. A uniform illuminance distribution is usually defined as one where the minimum illuminance is not less than 0.8 of the average, excluding a band 0.5 m wide around the edge of the room. The uniformity requirement will normally be achieved if the manufacturer's recommended SHR_{nom} is not exceeded. However, because the SHR_{nom} is given at set values (for example 0.5, 0.75, 1.0,...), a separate maximum value may also be provided; this is the maximum spacing possible for uniform illumination with that luminaire.

4   Calculate the number of luminaires required:

$$N = \frac{E_s\, A}{F\, n\, MF\, UF} \qquad\qquad (16.8)$$

where N is the number of luminaires necessary to produce an average illuminance of E_s lux across a horizontal reference plane of area of A m^2. The value n is the number of lamps per luminaire, and F defines the initial lamp lumen output: that is, when the lamps are new or, in the case of discharge lamps, after a burning time of 100 hours. UF is the utilization factor for the luminaire, and MF is the maintenance factor based on the luminaire and lamp type, and the cleanliness of the room atmosphere.

Example

How many luminaires, of the type shown on page 160, are required to give 500 lx over the whole horizontal working plane in the office illustrated in Figure 16.1? Adopt a working plane height of 0.8 m above the floor.

The luminaires are to be ceiling mounted and equipped with two 1.2 m long, 36 W, T8 (25 mm tube diameter) fluorescent lamps, which have an initial lamp light output of 3350 lm. Because the room is daylit for much of the time, and the electric lighting needs to complement it when necessary, a lamp with an 'intermediate' correlated colour temperature of 4000 K has been selected. Also, because the occupants will be involved in tasks that have a colour assessment component, the lamps need to have a colour rendering index (R_a) of not less than 80. For the purpose of the example assume that the maintenance factor to produce the maintained illuminance after 6000 hours (approximately two years for an office) is 0.8.

Room index, using equation (16.7):

$$K = \frac{4.0 \times 8.0}{(4.0 + 8.0) \times (3.0 - 0.8)} = 1.2$$

The room reflectances are given in Example (c) above: ceiling 0.7, walls 0.4, floor 0.2. We adopt the floor reflectance as the reflectance of the working plane. Then, from the utilization factor table on page 160, $UF = 0.53$.

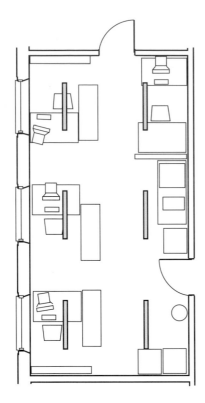

Figure 16.9 *Luminaire positions for maximum illuminance uniformity. These would cause reflections of luminaires in desktops.*

Reflectances in the left-hand column of the table are given as percentages. The final utilization factor is given by interpolation between wall reflectance of 30% and 50% and also between room indices of 1.00 and 1.25.

Equation (16.8) can now be used to give the number of luminaires required:

$$N = \frac{500 \times 4.0 \times 8.0}{3350 \times 2 \times 0.8 \times 0.53} = 5.6$$

The designer now has to decide whether there should be five or six luminaires. Since the room lends itself to a rectangular array of luminaires, six luminaires rather than five should be used in a two-by-three array, as shown in Figure 16.9.

Now check to ensure that the centre-to-centre luminaire spacing, S, does not exceed the recommended ratio of spacing to mounting height. For even illumination, the distance from a luminaire to the adjacent wall should be half the centre-to-centre spacing.

$$\frac{S}{h_m} \text{ (lengthwise)} = \frac{8.0}{3 \times 2.2} = 1.2$$

$$\frac{S}{h_m} \text{ (widthwise)} = \frac{4.0}{2 \times 2.2} = 0.9$$

Since both these ratios are less than 1.36 (the SHR_{max} value given in the table for a square array), the uniformity of working plane illuminance would be satisfactory.

Comment

Although this luminaire layout is the best for the evenness of working-plane illuminance, the fittings may give glaring reflections in shiny desktop surfaces (see Chapter 9). A compromise is needed, and a better solution is given by moving the rows of luminaires closer to the centre-line of the room to avoid the 'offending zones' above the desks. Even then, problems could occur: if the tables to the sides of the desks are critical task areas, specular reflections here would be unacceptable. In this case either another furniture layout or a different type of room lighting might be necessary.

The installation would provide the required task illuminance, but the designer still needs to assess that the light distribution around the room is acceptable. When there is no daylight, with this installation there would be little light on the walls and only reflected light on the ceiling. Ceiling and wall illuminance can be estimated from the polar curve and the upward light output ratio (ULOR), which show that there is no upward light from the luminaire, and from the *UF* for a zero reflectance room, which shows that about

80% of the downward light from this installation goes directly onto the floor cavity, leaving less than 20% to light the walls.

The lumen method calculation is based on an empty room. If a room is to be furnished with tall furniture such as filing cabinets or partitions, these need to be taken into account by a reduction in the adopted *UF* value.

To use the electric lighting to complement the daylight in an energy-efficient way the row of luminaires nearer the window should be separately switched. This is considered in the next section.

(e) ESTIMATING ENERGY USE

Purpose

Energy efficiency in lighting is important because most of the electricity it consumes, particularly in the developed world, is generated by burning fossil fuels – oil, coal and gas. This produces atmospheric pollution, mainly by carbon dioxide emissions, which cause environmental damage and climate changes that lead to global warming. Energy efficiency reduces users' operating costs, and energy-saving schemes are usually economically worthwhile within the lifetime costs of the installation

Method

1 Find (from the manufacturer's catalogue) the circuit wattage of the lamp and its control equipment, P_c watts.

2 Calculate the installed power density of the installation:

$$P_{id} = \frac{100N\,P_c}{E_s\,A} \quad \text{W}/\text{m}^2/100\,\text{lux} \qquad (16.9)$$

where N is the number of luminaires, E_s is the maintained illuminance, and A is the illuminated area (usually the working plane area).

Compare this with recommended or required values for the type of installation.

3 Estimate the total annual operating time, T_{annual} hours, and the unit cost of electricity, C. In the UK, cost is measured in pounds sterling per kilowatt-hour, £/kWh.

4 Calculate annual cost of electricity:

$$C_{annual} = N\,P_c\,T_{annual}\,C/1000 \qquad (16.10)$$

Example

We continue Example (d), examining the choice of lamp control equipment.

A twin 1.2 m 36 W fluorescent lamp luminaire with wire-wound control gear consumes 90 W or 0.09 kW (lamps and control gear). The installed power density is therefore

$$P_{id} = \frac{100 \times 6 \times 90}{500 \times 32} = 3.375 \text{ W/ m}^2 \text{ /100lux}$$

The *CIBSE Code for Interior Lighting* suggests, for a room of this type, a target range of installed power density: 2.7 to 5.4 W/m²/ 100 lx. The calculated value lies in the middle of this range, and is reasonable by present standards. However, a twin 1.2 m 36 W fluorescent lamp luminaire with electronic high-frequency control gear consumes 72 W for the same light output. This would be much better, giving an installed power density of 2.7 W/m²/100 lx, a value at the bottom of the *CIBSE Code* range.

If the lights are switched on for 10 hours per day for 250 days in the year, T_{annual} = 2500 hours. Then if, for example, the unit cost of electricity is 0.07 £/kWh, the annual cost of the power used in the installation with wire-wound control gear is

$$C_{annual} = 6 \times 0.09 \times 2500 \times 0.07 = £94.50$$

With electronic control gear the annual cost would £75.60. The capital cost of this installation would be higher, but typically, at present prices, the payback period of this cost difference would be less than three years. That is, for an installation lifetime longer than three years, the 20% reduction in annual power cost would have an economic advantage in addition to the general environmental gain.

Now consider the daylighting performance. At the desks near the windows, the point daylight factor is approximately 10% (Figure 16.8). Equation (5.3) in Chapter 5 relates internal illuminance to external diffuse illuminance:

$$E = \frac{D f_o E_{dh}}{100\%} \tag{5.3}$$

where D is the daylight factor, f_o is an orientation factor, and E_{dh} is the external illuminance.

For a west-facing room, f_o = 1.2 (from the graph given in section (i), page 158).

Rearranging equation (5.3), the external diffuse illuminance corresponding with a 10% daylight factor is therefore

$$E_{dh} = \frac{500 \times 100}{10 \times 1.2} = 4167\,\mathrm{lx} = 4.167\,\mathrm{klx}$$

It can be seen in the daylight availability graph, page 158, that this external illuminance is on average exceeded for approximately 70% of annual hours between 9.00 and 19.00. Therefore if the row of luminaires nearer the windows could be controlled to respond perfectly to daylight availability, there would be a 70% power saving in that part of the installation. However, considering the daylight factor of 1% on the desktop at the back of the room, it can be seen that the corresponding external illuminance of 41.67 klx is achieved for less than 10% of annual working hours. This suggests that electric lighting at the back of the room would normally be switched on during the working day.

Comment

To achieve energy savings with daylighting the luminaires must be controlled to respond to the daylight, and this must be done in a way that is acceptable to occupants.

The simplest form of control is manual switching. It is essential that the row of lights nearer the window is on a separate circuit from the rear row, or the whole installation will be switched on whenever extra illumination is needed in the darker parts of the room. Basic automatic control could be achieved by the use of a photoelectric sensor, but, to ensure that automatic switching does not cause a distraction, switching *off* should occur at an illuminance where this would hardly be noticed – for example about 1500 lx total (daylight plus electric light) when the design illuminance is 500 lx. To ensure that the users feel that they have control, a manual override should be provided.

Chapters 6 and 14 discuss further the requirements of lighting control.

(f) THE POINT SOURCE FORMULA: DIRECT ILLUMINANCE FROM A SMALL LUMINAIRE

Purpose

A lighting designer often needs to calculate illuminance from a small source, such as a ceiling-mounted downlight luminaire shining on a table, or a spotlight illuminating a picture. The point source method gives the direct illuminance: the light that arrives without reflection from any other surface.

A **point source** of light is one that is small compared with the distance from the luminaire to the surface it illuminates. Usually this is taken to be a source that has a maximum dimension of one-fifth of the distance between the source and the surface.

Method

The point source formula is given in Chapter 1 (equation (1.2) and Figure 1.3):

$$E = \frac{I \cos \theta}{d^2} \tag{1.2}$$

where E is the illuminance (lux) at a point on a surface, I is the luminous intensity (candelas) in the direction from the source to the surface point, θ is the angle (degrees) between the source direction and the normal to the surface at the point, and d is the distance (metres) from source to point.

When several values are to be tabulated, the equation is sometimes written

$$E_{(P)} = \frac{I_{(\phi)} \cos \theta}{d^2} \tag{16.11}$$

where P is the surface point under consideration, and ϕ is the angle between the beam axis of the luminaire and the direction from the luminaire to the surface point.

If the source is a perpendicular distance h above a surface:

$$d = \frac{h}{\cos \theta}$$

and therefore the formula can take the form

$$E_{(P)} = \frac{I_{(\phi)} \cos^3 \theta}{h^2} \tag{16.12}$$

The combined effect of several sources is obtained by adding individual illuminances together.

Example

Determine the illuminance at points A and B on a horizontal plane 3 m beneath a ceiling-recessed downlight luminaire. Point A is under the luminaire centre and point B is 1 m to the side of A; see Figure 16.10. The luminaire is equipped with three 26 W

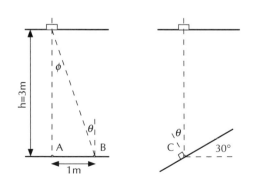

Figure 16.10 *Illuminance from a point source.*

compact fluorescent lamps with a total lumen output of 5400 lm. The luminaire has a symmetrical luminous intensity distribution: that is, the intensity is the same in all vertical planes through the centre of the luminaire, and is symmetrical about the vertical centre line.

Section (i), page 161, shows a typical intensity distribution for this type of luminaire. The first column of the table gives the angle ϕ (from vertical downwards) at which the intensity is measured. The second column shows intensity in candelas per 1000 lumens of lamp light output: this is a common technique used by luminaire manufacturers to avoid printing similar data for a luminaire that has different lamp type possibilities. The third column of the table gives absolute intensity values: that is, the second column values multiplied by 5.4 (5400/1000). This information is also presented graphically as a polar curve.

Illuminance at point A:

From the data sheet, the intensity vertically downwards ($\phi = 0°$) is 1566 cd; $\theta = 0°$; $d = 3$ m. Then, using equation (16.10):

$$E_{(A)} = \frac{I_{(\phi)} \cos\theta}{d^2} = \frac{1566 \cos\theta}{3^2} = 174\,\text{lux}$$

Illuminance at point B:

Here θ and ϕ are both 18.4°. Interpolating from the table, $I_{(18.4°)} = 1556$ cd so, using equation (16.12):

$$E_{(B)} = \frac{1556 \cos^3 18.4°}{3^2} = 148\,\text{lux}$$

Illuminance on a sloping surface:

If the surface is tilted by 30° (point C in Figure 16.10) the illuminance directly below the luminaire is given by equation (16.10) with $\theta = 30°$.

$$E_{(C)} = \frac{1566 \cos 30°}{3^2} = 151\,\text{lux}$$

Comment

Point illuminance calculations can be used to produce isolux diagrams – contours of equal illuminance from a luminaire mounted at a given height above a surface. If they are drawn to scale, isolux diagrams can be superimposed on the floor plan of a building to show directly the light received from light fittings in specific positions. Isolux diagrams do, of course, show only direct illuminance; interreflected light in a room is not included. Figure 16.11 shows an isolux diagram for the downlight luminaire used.

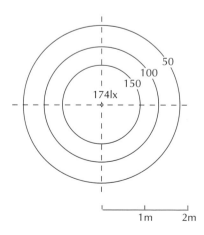

Figure 16.11 *Isolux diagram for the luminaire used in Example (f). The mounting height is 3 m.*

The calculations in the examples above have been made for new lamps: that is, the initial lamp lumen output has been used. If a value for maintained illuminance is required then a maintenance factor has to be included to take into account light loss due to dirt and lamp lumen depreciation.

Direct illuminance calculations are sometimes required for luminaires that are not point sources, such as linear fluorescent fittings. This can be done by assuming that the luminaire is divided into a number of equal segments, each of a size that can be classed as a point source. The direct illuminance from each segment is then calculated, with different distances and angles for the different segments, and the results added up give the illuminance from the whole source. This technique assumes that each segment has the same relative intensity distribution but that the flux output is proportional to the segment size. For example, if a 1500 mm luminaire is divided into six parts, each segment is taken to have the same intensity distribution but to give only one-sixth of the flux output. This technique is commonly used in computer calculations. The approach can also be used for area sources.

Various theoretical formulae exist for calculating illuminance from line and area sources.

(g) ACCENT LIGHTING: WHICH SPOTLIGHT?

Purpose

Accent lighting (or spotlighting) provides visual emphasis by highlighting an object. Used particularly for decorative purposes, it might enhance a company logo in a reception area, a display in a retail outlet, or a flower arrangement in a hotel lobby. It can also be used for functional purposes, enhancing visibility by making the object stand out from the background. Spotlights often provide the main illumination for exhibits in museums and art galleries.

Spotlights come in a variety of forms. Some are little more than a reflector lamp in a housing that incorporates a means of supporting the lamp and connecting it to the supply, while others use a small light source in a complex optical system. Spotlights are adjustable in terms of their aiming angle. They can be surface mounted or recessed into a ceiling; they can also be mounted onto a track system, which provides an electrical supply through one or more different circuits – this allows flexibility in the positioning and aiming of luminaires, and is particularly useful where different display positions are required. Some spotlights allow attachments to be incorporated, such as supplementary optics for shaping the beam, barn-doors or louvres for masking spill-light. Colour filters and projection slides, called gobos, can also be used for special effects. Spotlights that incorporate small motors are available, allowing aiming positions to be changed remotely or animated lighting displays to be provided.

The light sources most commonly used are low-voltage tungsten–halogen lamps. They have excellent colour performance, they can be dimmed, they have a life of typically 2000–3000 hours, and (for an incandescent source) their energy efficiency is reasonable. Some lamps incorporate their own basic optics, with a wide range of different beam intensities and shapes to choose from. Alternatively, small capsule versions can be used in luminaires that incorporate optics; in some cases these are adjustable, allowing different beam sizes to be obtained from a single unit.

Alternative sources for spotlights are the comparatively recently developed small metal halide lamps. These provide good colour performance, have a typical minimum life of 5000 hours, and give good energy efficiency. However, they cannot be dimmed, and they take a few minutes to reach full light output.

A form of spotlighting that is gaining in popularity is the fibre-optic system, which can employ either a tungsten–halogen or a metal halide source. The lamp is housed remotely from the outlets, and the light is transported by bundles of optical fibres. There can be several outlets for each lamp, and these can be fitted with any of a range of different optics. The lamp housing can be positioned for easy maintenance, good heat control can be achieved, and the sizes of the fibre-optic outlets can be very small. However, the overall efficiency is low, and if the optical fibres are too long the colour of the light is distorted. Fibre-optic systems are especially useful in lighting display cases.

Method

1 Select the spotlight location. Some experimentation may be necessary. A common technique is to aim the spotlight at an angle of about 30–45° to the downward vertical, as in Figure 16.12; this can provide a 'natural' pattern of modelling.

2 Select the beam size needed. If the area to be lit is large, or the distance between the light source and the display is small, several spotlights with overlapping beams may be required. Check spill light into the eyes of viewers and onto other surfaces around the display. To avoid visual discomfort and glare, spotlights often require louvres or some form of masking. Consider the beam cut-off and whether this should have a hard or soft edge.

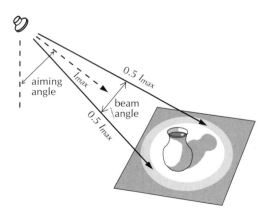

Figure 16.12 *Aiming and beam angles of a spotlight.*

3 Determine the required illuminance on the object. This can depend on the background illuminance and the degree of visual impact required (see Chapter 11).

4 Either:

use the point source formula given in Example (f), rearranged to give the **luminous intensity**:

$$I = \frac{E\,d^2}{\cos\theta} \qquad (16.13)$$

then use the calculated intensity and required beam characteristics to select lamps and luminaires from manufacturers' data;

or:

Select the lamp and luminaire from manufacturers' **illuminance** data.

Photometric performance data of spotlights are usually presented by equipment manufacturers in one of two ways:

- an intensity distribution, given as a polar curve or a table;
- a beam or cone diagram. This gives the beam angle, which, for a symmetrical beam, is twice the angle between the direction of maximum intensity and the direction in which the intensity is half the maximum (see Figure 16.12). The information may be supplemented with the diameter of the beam at different distances. The diagram may also give the maximum illuminance at the centre of the beam and the illuminance at the edge of the beam (the 0.5 I_{max} position), for different distances between the spotlight and the object. These illuminance values are for a surface at 90° to the beam centre. If the beam is aimed at an angle, the illuminance must be multiplied by cos θ, where θ is the angle of incidence, as before.

Page 161 gives beam and intensity data for some low-voltage reflector lamps.

Note that, except for spotlights with a highly focused beam, there is some light outside the main beam. The rate at which the light reduces is described by the luminaire's intensity distribution; the hardness of the apparent edge is an important factor in the effect produced. Furthermore, illuminance across a beam is rarely uniform. Usually this does not matter as long as the effect is appropriate and the average illuminance is acceptable.

Example A

Spotlighting is required to highlight a floral display in a hotel lobby. The general illumination is about 200 lx on a horizontal plane. Table 11.1 (Chapter 11) suggests that for an object : background contrast that is significant without being too dramatic the illuminance ratio needs to be about 5 : 1. In this example, therefore, the object illuminance should be approximately 1000 lx, so an additional illuminance of 800 lx is required from accent lighting. We shall select a spotlight that achieves this on a horizontal plane at the position of the flowers.

The display is 600 mm across, and is to be lit from a ceiling-recessed luminaire with an aiming angle of 30°. The ceiling is 3 m above the display (Figure 16.13). The distance between the spotlight and the display is approximately 3.5 m. With a 600 mm diameter display this requires a beam angle of approximately 10°.

Applying equation (16.13):

$$I = \frac{800 \times 3.5^2}{\cos 3\theta} = 11316 \, cd$$

Choosing from the lamps listed on page 161, the nearest option is a 50 W narrow-beam spotlight (beam angle 10°), which has a maximum intensity of 11 500 cd.

Example B

A small commercial art gallery requires a system of adjustable spotlighting to illuminate paintings hung at normal eye height, 1.5 m above floor level. The ceiling height is 3 m above floor level. The paintings form temporary exhibitions, and vary in height from about 300 mm to 700 mm. Since there is need for flexibility, a ceiling-mounted track system is proposed, together with a range of spotlight types to accommodate the range of painting sizes. The track system will be positioned to allow an aiming angle, at the centre of the picture, of 35° from the downward vertical (see Figure 16.14). This will ensure that reflected light emerges outside the normal viewing position. The distance between the spotlight and the centre of the picture is approximately 1.8 m and, for the range of picture sizes given, this implies beam angles from 10° to 24°. Pictures that are wider than their height require more than one spotlight, with overlapping beams.

A 20 W spotlight with a 10° beam angle would provide an illuminance at the centre of the picture of

$$E = \frac{5000 \times \cos(90 - 35)}{1.8^2} = 885 \, lx$$

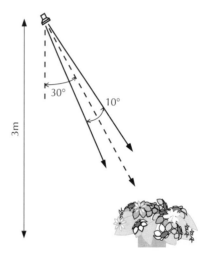

Figure 16.13 *Spotlight calculation example A.*

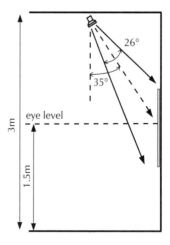

Figure 16.14 *Spotlight calculation example B.*

A 50 W spotlight with a 24° beam angle has the same peak intensity, and would provide the same illuminance at the centre, but with a greater beam width.

Comment

When accent lighting is used for purposes such as Example A, a commonsense view should be taken of the degree of accuracy required. The aim is solely to select the most appropriate luminaire, and an experienced designer might do this without calculation. For a gallery (Example B), the situation can be different. It is sometimes important to control accurately the illuminance on pictures, not only to achieve a satisfactory brightness pattern in the room as a whole but also to limit the light exposure of exhibits. When illuminance is considered to be too high, it can be reduced by using neutral density filters in the beam. Dimming can be used only if a slight change in the colour appearance of the light is acceptable.

(h) WALLS AND CEILINGS

Purpose

So far we have considered task lighting, particularly on a horizontal plane, and the illumination of decorative objects. But, as we have seen in Chapter 7, the overall appearance of a room depends on all its surfaces, especially the walls and ceiling. To create an attractively lit interior it is often necessary to design electric lighting specifically to illuminate these areas. In addition, it is sometimes necessary to illuminate room surfaces for functional purposes: for instance, to increase the visibility of a decorated ceiling, a wall painting or a bookstack in a library. The final examples in this chapter describe some techniques, without calculations, for wall and ceiling lighting.

Vertical surfaces are important because they form a major part of the normal field of view. Lighting the walls of a space clearly defines its perimeter, and helps to give the room a 'light' appearance. Illumination of the ceiling, either directly or just by reflection, also helps to create a sense of lightness. It avoids the upper part of the room being perceived as heavy and oppressive: interiors that have little light on the ceiling can be gloomy. However, if all the surfaces are lit uniformly the space is likely to appear bland. The aim should be to compose a pattern of light and shade that responds to the architectural form of the space, and to the finish and texture of its surfaces. It is vital to plan a hierarchy of brightness that is meaningful for the space. A wall or ceiling is too bright if it appears unnatural or attracts the eye for no good purpose.

Lighting vertical surfaces

If the wall is to be lit for functional reasons then the required task illuminance is a good starting point. The task also then determines the required illuminance distribution: remember, for good visibility a task should have the highest illuminance relative to its immediate surroundings. However, if a wall is to be lit for decorative purposes in a space that has normal working illuminances of 300–500 lx, an average luminance of at least 30 cd/m² is necessary to create a sense of lightness.

The next consideration is the wall surface finish – smooth or textured? If it is smooth and lit obliquely, the light shows up any imperfections in the surface. If, however, it is textured and *not* lit obliquely, then much of the textured effect will be lost. The perception of illuminance variation across a surface also depends on the texture and on the colour and pattern. For a smooth wall of one colour the target for illuminance diversity is often quite small, typically in the range 2 : 1 to 5 : 1; for a rough or multicoloured wall the corresponding diversity criterion tends to lie between 5 : 1 and 10 : 1.

There are two basic techniques for lighting vertical surfaces. The first involves the use of linear systems with either hot- or cold-cathode fluorescent lamps. If the system is installed horizontally and parallel to the wall, a continuous up/down gradation of light is created, as shown in Figures 16.15 and 16.16; conversely, vertical mounting gives a gradation along the length of the wall.

If linear fluorescent lamps are installed end to end, dark patches should be avoided by overlapping the ends of the tubes or by mounting them very close together but as far as possible from the surface. Cold-cathode fluorescent lamps are often used for wall illumination because they can be made in long continuous strips, and bent if required to fit curved walls or special shapes. They can be manufactured with the ends turned back through 180° so that the illuminated part of the lamps can be butted close together to avoid dark shadows.

The second technique is to use small light sources, spaced uniformly and parallel to the surface, as in Figure 16.17. This tends to create a scalloped pattern of light. The degree of patterning depends on the luminaire's intensity distribution and the luminaire spacing relative to the distance from the surface: the smaller this spacing-to-distance ratio, the less evident the pattern.

Rooms can be illuminated by using individual wall-mounted lights, a technique often used in corridors and in interiors such as hotel lounges. The locations of the sources in relation to the surface depend on the specific luminaires used and on the effect required. It is important in lighting of this type to screen the lamp from normal directions of view, although in some special cases glimpses of the

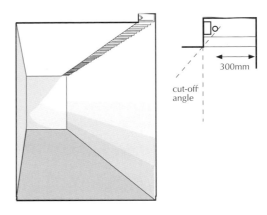

Figure 16.15 *Wall lighting with recessed cornice strip.*

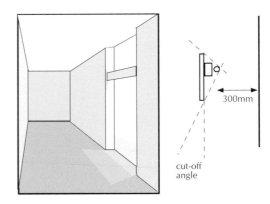

Figure 16.16 *Wall lighting with pelmet*

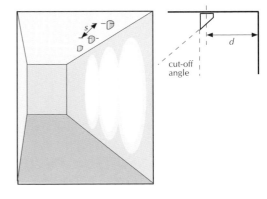

Figure 16.17 *Wall lighting with asymmetric luminaires. The ratio s/d indicates illuminance uniformity.*

lamp can be used to create sparkle. These glimpses, however, must be tiny, otherwise glare and visual discomfort result.

With all surface lighting installations, the level and distribution of illuminance and the related luminance pattern depend on the light output of the lamps, the optical performance of the luminaire, and the reflectance of the illuminated surfaces. When designing, a good first step is to draw a shaded sketch, composing a hierarchy of brightnesses, which sets the wall into the context of the whole interior. From these brightnesses, estimates can be made first of the required luminances, and then of the corresponding illuminances. Practice is necessary to develop skill in this approach, but the actual illuminance values are not critical. It is achieving the hierarchy that is crucial, determining which surfaces are to be brightest and which are secondary.

In some cases standard catalogue luminaires are appropriate, and then the manufacturer normally provides illumination performance data. If, however, it is decided to use lamps incorporated into building features it can be difficult to determine the lighting performance accurately. Mock-ups can be used when accurate values are needed, but simple calculations can give useful estimates of illuminance.

To illuminate walls with a satisfactory degree of uniformity, it is necessary either to mount the lamps a reasonable distance from the surface (usually not less than 300 mm) or to incorporate optical elements such as linear reflectors or prismatic plates, which create an asymmetric intensity distribution. It is a common fault that this aspect of wall lighting is inadequately considered and that lamps are placed too close to the wall. The result is a very patchy distribution: beware! Finally, check cut-off angles of all lamps to ensure that they can not be seen from normal directions of view.

Lighting ceilings

Interiors are sometimes lit with indirect lighting luminaires or **uplighters**. For task illuminance this can be inefficient, because light reaches the normal working plane only by reflection; luminaires with a very high light output ratio and high efficacy sources are needed if the result is to be worthwhile.

A room lit primarily with uplighters has two important visual characteristics: the reflected illumination on a horizontal working plane is very uniform, sometimes giving virtually shadowless lighting; and the ceiling is bright in relation to other room surfaces – it can be over-bright when a high task illuminance is required. However, background illumination from uplighters complemented with direct local task lighting can be efficient and visually attractive.

The brightness distribution on the ceiling from uplighters needs careful consideration. The luminaire intensity distribution must ensure that a graded pattern of luminance is produced – a luminance distribution that fades away gradually and up again into the next patch of light. An installation that creates 'hot-spots' on the ceiling or a very contrasty pattern of brightness is unattractive and distracting. This effect is worse if the ceiling is finished in a non-matt material: it is essential for the ceiling to have a high-reflectance matt surface.

Uplighters can be suspended from the ceiling, wall mounted or free-standing on the floor. In all cases the lamp must be screened from normal directions of view. The top of the luminaire must be protected with a cover glass, to aid maintenance and to avoid a build-up of dirt in the luminaire, which reduces light output and can be a fire hazard.

A range of uplighter luminaires is available. Sometimes the photometric performance is provided by the manufacturer in the form of an isolux diagram, which can be used as an illumination 'footprint' over the plan of the space to determine the illuminance distribution. Alternatively, if the luminaires are to be used in a regular array then a utilization factor may be provided, which can be used in the lumen method given in Example (d).

Other than specific uplighters, there are several other ways in which light can be thrown onto the ceiling to alleviate gloominess. Many standard luminaires have an upward component to their output; as discussed in Example (d) this can be indicated by the luminaire's polar curve of intensity and also by the upward light output ratio (ULOR) found in its tabulated photometric data. Adequate light in a room may also be reflected upwards from the floor cavity, if this is of sufficiently high reflectance. Ceiling light can also be provided by using architectural features to house luminaires.

Lamps within such architectural elements are often linear sources, usually fluorescent types. They can be incorporated into coves or cornices, but the lamps must be placed so that a soft gradually changing light pattern is produced. For this, a cornice must be sufficiently below the ceiling for light to be projected a reasonable distance across the ceiling surface. As a rule of thumb, the distance that the light is projected across the ceiling is about five times the distance of the cornice below the ceiling. Asymmetric reflectors can help. The light pattern can also be improved by radiusing the corner between the wall and ceiling, as illustrated in Figure 16.18. As with wall lighting, the ends of linear lamps must be close to each other, to avoid casting dark shadows.

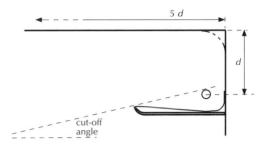

Figure 16.18 *Ceiling lighting using a cornice. The ceiling is illuminated for a distance approximately 5d.*

(i) DATA

Sky diagrams

Vertical sky component overlay

When placed on a stereographic drawing of obstructions to daylight, each V-point lying on unobstructed sky represents 0.25 D_{sv} (the actual point lies at the vertex of each V). The overlay should be rotated so that the arrow lies in the direction faced by the vertical surface.

Base for stereographic drawings

This is used to plot obstructions to daylight at a point on a site or inside a building. The centre is the zenith, the perimeter circle is the horizon. The angles around the perimeter are directions of azimuth, measured from north; for example, east lies at 90°.

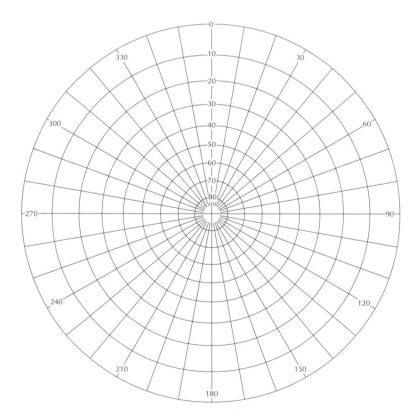

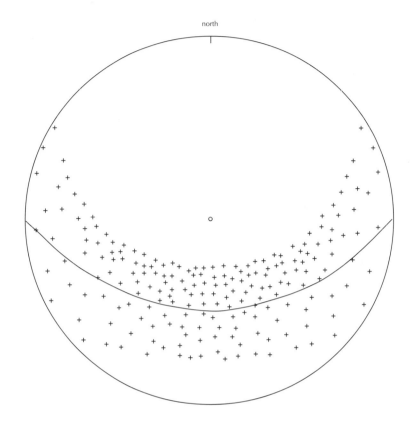

Probable sunlight hours overlay for London

Each point represents 0.5 T_{ps} in London but the diagram may be applied for block design purposes to sites in England and Wales generally. The curved line is the equinox sunpath.

Stereographic sunpath diagram for London

The sunpaths are drawn for solar time at a latitude of 51° north. Taking into account normal standards of accuracy in plotting obstructions, the diagram may be used for sites lying between 48° and 54° latitude.

Daylight availability

Daylight availability in London

The upper graph gives cumulative daylight availability. It is the average percentage of annual hours that a particular value of external diffuse illuminance is exceeded. For normal daylight estimation purposes, this graph may be applied generally to sites in southern England.

The lower graph gives the orientation factor for diffuse illuminance, relating the actual diffuse sky illuminance for windows facing in a particular direction to the illuminance that would be received from a CIE overcast sky. For normal daylight estimation purposes, this graph may be applied to other daytime working hours and to other parts of Britain

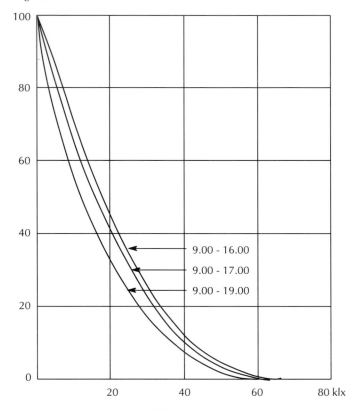

% of working year exceeded for given working hours

9.00 - 16.00
9.00 - 17.00
9.00 - 19.00

E_{dh}, diffuse horizontal illuminance in London

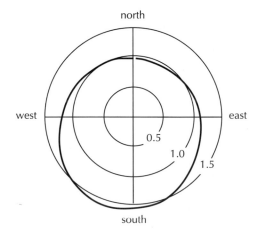

f_o, mean diffuse illuminance orientation factor for London, 9.00 - 17.00 working day

Typical reflectances under diffuse daylight

Ground:		Carpet (cream)	0.4
Snow (new)	0.8	Wood (light veneers)	0.4
Sand	0.3	Wood (medium colours)	0.2
Paving	0.2	Wood (dark)	0.1
Earth (dry)	0.2	Quarry tiles	0.1
Earth (moist)	0.1	Window glass	0.1
Green vegetation	0.1	Carpet (deep colours)	0.1

Other external materials:		Paint colours, with Munsell ref:	
White glazed tile	0.7	White N9.5	0.85
Portland stone	0.6	Pale cream 5Y9/2	0.81
Medium limestone	0.4	Light grey N8.5	0.68
Concrete	0.4	Strong yellow 6.25Y8.5/13	0.64
Brickwork (buff)	0.3	Mid-grey N7	0.45
Brickwork (red)	0.2	Strong green 5G5/10	0.22
Granite	0.2	Strong red 7.5R4.5/16	0.18
Window glass	0.1	Strong blue 10B4/10	0.15
Tree foliage	0.1	Dark grey 5Y4/0.5	0.14
		Dark brown 10Y3/6	0.10
Materials used internally:		Deep red-purple 7.5RP3/6	0.10
White paper	0.8	Black N1.5	0.05
Stainless steel	0.4		
Cement screed	0.4		

Transmittance of windows

The transparency of materials to radiation depends on the wavelength, so the transmittance of light differs from the average for all solar radiation and also from the transmittances of the infrared and the ultraviolet. In addition, transmittance depends on the angle of incidence: it is greatest when the incident beam is perpendicular to the surface and zero when the beam is at glancing incidence. For diffuse daylight calculations it is the **diffuse transmittance** that is required, the weighted mean transmittance over all angles of incidence. This is always less than the normal transmittance. Manufacturer's literature must be read with care because the type of transmittance values listed is not always made clear.

Glazing transmittance is also affect by dirt, so the clean transmittance values may have to be multiplied by a maintenance factor. Some values for this are given in Table 14.3.

Approximate diffuse transmittance of clean glazing:

Clear single glazing	0.8
Clear double glazing	0.7
Low emissivity double glazing	0.65

Typical utilization factors

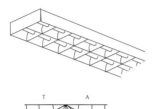

These represent a luminaire with two 1.2 m 36 W fluorescent lamps and mirror louvred optical control. The table is based on an example in the *CIBSE Code for interior lighting*.

Nadir intensity	302 cd/1000 lm
CIE flux code	68 99 100 100 64
SHR_{max} (square)	1.36
$SHR_{max\,tr}$ (continuous rows)	1.75
ULOR (upward light output ratio)	0.00
DLOR (downward light output ratio)	0.64
LOR (light output ratio)	0.64
CIBSE LG3 category	3

Correction factors:

	36 W	58 W	32 W	50 W
Length factor	1.00	1.00	1.00	1.00
HF factor			1.01	1.01

Utilization factors UF_F for SHR_{nom} of 1.25:

Room reflectance			Room index, K								
C	W	F	0.75	1.00	1.25	1.50	2.00	2.50	3.00	4.00	5.00
70	50	20	0.45	0.51	0.56	0.58	0.62	0.64	0.66	0.68	0.69
	30		0.41	0.48	0.52	0.55	0.59	0.62	0.64	0.66	0.68
	10		0.38	0.45	0.49	0.53	0.57	0.60	0.62	0.65	0.66
50	50	20	0.44	0.50	0.54	0.57	0.60	0.62	0.64	0.65	0.67
	30		0.40	0.47	0.51	0.54	0.58	0.60	0.62	0.64	0.65
	10		0.38	0.44	0.49	0.52	0.56	0.58	0.60	0.63	0.64
30	50	20	0.43	0.49	0.53	0.55	0.58	0.60	0.62	0.63	0.64
	30		0.40	0.46	0.50	0.53	0.56	0.59	0.60	0.62	0.63
	10		0.37	0.44	0.48	0.51	0.55	0.57	0.59	0.61	0.62
0	0	0	0.36	0.43	0.47	0.49	0.53	0.55	0.56	0.58	0.59

Typical luminous intensity data

Ceiling-recessed circular luminaire, 0.3 m diameter, with three 26 W compact fluorescent lamps having a total light output of 5400 lm.

Actual manufacturer's data should be used for lighting calculations in practice.

Intensity angle from vertical, ϕ (degrees)	Luminous intensity (cd/1000 lm)	Luminous intensity (cd)
0	290	1566
5	295	1593
10	300	1620
15	295	1593
20	285	1539
25	250	1350
30	210	1134
35	180	972
40	150	810
45	80	432
50	50	270
55	0	0

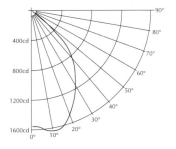

Peak intensities and beam angles of low-voltage reflector spotlights

Spotlight beam description	Watts	Peak luminous intensity (cd)	Beam angle (degrees)
Narrow	20	5000	10
Wide	20	700	38
Very wide	20	350	60
Narrow	50	11500	10
Medium	50	5000	24
Wide	50	2000	38

(j) REFERENCES AND FURTHER READING

This list gives further sources of data, some of the principal codes and design guides for lighting, and a number of books that are either good introductions to lighting generally or more detailed studies of particular topics.

Guides and standards

Code for interior lighting (1994), Chartered Institution of Building Services Engineers, London.

Lighting handbook: reference and application, 8th edn. Illuminating Engineering Society of North America, New York.

A guide to good urban lighting: lighting the environment (1995), Institution of Lighting Engineers and Chartered Institution of Building Services Engineers, London.

BS 4800 *Schedule of paint colours for building purposes,* British Standards Institution, London.

BS 8206 *Lighting for buildings: Part 2: Code of practice for daylighting,* British Standards Institution, London.

CIBSE Lighting Guides, Chartered Institution of Building Services Engineers, London:

LG1 (1989)*The industrial environment.*
LG2 (1989)*Hospitals and health care buildings.*
LG3 (1996)*The visual environment for display screen use.*
LG4 (1990)*Sports.*
LG5 (1991)*The visual environment in lecture, teaching and conference rooms.*
LG6 (1992)*The outdoor environment.*
LG7 (1993)*Lighting for offices.*
LG8 (1994) *Museums and art galleries.*

CIBSE Technical Memoranda: Chartered Institution of Building Services Engineers, London:

TM5 (1980) *The calculation and use of utilization factors.*
TM12 (1986)*Emergency lighting.*

BRE publications: Building Research Establishment, Garston:

BRE Digests 309 & 310 *Estimating daylight in buildings: Parts 1 and 2.*
BR209 (1991) Littlefair, P. J. *Site layout planning for daylight and sunlight: a guide to good practice.*
BR288 (1995) Bell, J. A. M. and Burt, W. *Designing buildings for daylight.*
BR305 (1996) Littlefair, P. J. *Designing with innovative daylight.*

Books

Baker, N., Fanchiotti, A. and Steemers, K. (eds.) (1993) *Daylighting in architecture: a European reference book.* James & James, London.

Boyce, P. R. (1981) *Human factors in lighting,* Applied Science, London.

Coaton, J. R. and Marsden, A. M. (1997) *Lamps and lighting,* 4th edn, Arnold, London.

Gardner, C. and Hannaford, B. (1983) *Lighting design,* The Design Council, London.

Hopkinson, R. G. and Collins, J. B. (1970) *The ergonomics of lighting,* Macdonald, London.

Hopkinson, R. G. Petherbridge, P. and Longmore, J. (1966) *Daylighting,* Heinemann, London.

Hunt, R. W. G. (1991) *Measuring colour,* 2nd edn, Ellis Horwood, New York.

Lam, W. M. C. (1977) *Perception and lighting as formgivers for architecture,* McGraw-Hill, New York.

Leslie, R. P and Rodgers, P. A. (1996) *The outdoor lighting pattern book,* McGraw-Hill, New York.

Lynes, J. A. (1968) *Principles of natural lighting,* Elsevier, London.

Lynes, J.A. and Bedöcs, L. (1996) *Lighting people and places – electric lighting for buildings.* Professional Studies in British Architectural Practice – Lighting. Royal Institute of British Architects & Thorn Lighting, London.

Michel, L. (1996) *Light: the shape of space,* Van Nostrand Reinhold, New York.

Millet, M. S. (1996) *Light revealing architecture,* Van Nostrand Reinhold, New York.

Moore, F. (1985) *Concepts and practice of architectural daylighting,* Van Nostrand Reinhold, New York.

Murdoch, J. B. (1985) *Illumination engineering – from Edison's lamp to the laser,* Macmillan, New York.

Pritchard, D. C. (1995) *Lighting,* 5th edn, Longman Scientific and Technical, Harlow.

Sobel, M. I. (1987) *Light,* University of Chicago Press, Chicago.

Steffy, G. R. (1990) *Architectural lighting design,* Van Nostrand Reinhold, New York.

Turner, J. (1994) *Lighting,* Batsford, London.

Index